ISAAC BABEL

In the same series:

Modern Literature Monographs

ISAAC BABEL

Richard Hallett

Frederick Ungar Publishing Co.
New York

891.73
B113H

First American edition, 1973

Copyright © 1972, 1973 by R. W. Hallett
Printed in the United States of America
Library of Congress Catalogue Card Number: 72–79939
Designed by Anita Duncan
ISBN: 0–8044–2337–7

Contents

88410

Chronology

1894:   13 July: Isaac Emmanuilovich Babel is born in Odessa.

1905–1911:   Studies at Nicholas I Commercial School in Odessa.

1911–1914:   Continues education in Kiev at the Institute of Financial and Business Studies, which moves to Saratov after war is declared.

1913:   Publishes "Old Shloyme" in Kiev.

1914–1915:   Completes his studies in Saratov.

1915:   Writes "Childhood: At Grandmother's."

1916:   Meets Maxim Gorky. "Mama, Rimma, and Alla" and "Il'ya Isaakovich and Margarita Prokof'yevna" appear in Gorky's journal. Publishes part of *Leaves from My Notebook*.

1917:   Volunteers for Russian army and is sent to Romanian front.

1918:   Is sent back to Odessa because of illness. Publishes *Diary*. Requisitions grain on the Volga during the summer.

1918–1919:   Works in the People's Commissariat for Education.

1919:   Marries Evgeniya Gronfeyn. Fights in the Northern Army.

1920:   Joins Budyonny's First Cavalry Army and fights in the Ukraine and Poland. Returns to Odessa at the end of the year.

1921:   Meets Konstantin Paustovsky. Publishes "The King."

1922:   Travels with his wife to the Caucasus and starts work on *Red Cavalry*.

1923:   His father, Emmanuel, dies. Babel publishes stories from *Red Cavalry*.

1924:   Returns to Odessa and then goes to Moscow. Publishes further stories from *Red Cavalry*.

1925:   February: Babel's sister goes to live in Brussels. He publishes "The Story of My Dovecote," "First Love," and new stories from *Red Cavalry*. His wife emigrates to Paris.

1926:   July: Babel's mother joins her daughter in Brussels. First publication of separate edition of *Red Cavalry*. Begins working in films.

1927:   July: travels to visit relatives in western Europe.

1928:   October: returns to the Soviet Union. Publishes the play, *Sunset*.

1929:   July: Babel's daughter, Nathalie, is born in Paris. Babel spends most of the year in the Ukraine.

1930:   Is cleared of the charge of giving a defamatory interview on the French Riviera. Tours the countryside for material on agricultural collectivization.

1932:   September: visits relatives in western Europe.

1933:   April–May: visits Gorky in Sorrento. August: returns to Soviet Union.

1934:   August: defends himself at First Congress of Soviet Writers.

1935:   March: publishes *Maria*. June: leaves for Paris. September: returns to Odessa.

1936:   Maxim Gorky dies. Again Babel defends his silence at a literary conference.

1937:   January: Antonina Pirozhkov bears Babel a daughter.

1938:   Publishes "The Trial," his last known story.

1939:   Babel is arrested.

1940:   Is tried by military court.

1941:   17 March: dies in captivity (cause of death unspecified).

1

*The Biography
of a Writer*

By the very nature of his profession an imaginative writer presents an extremely difficult problem for those wishing to record his biography. It is a problem not posed by any other human category and may be most conveniently expressed by asking simply: What is a writer's true biography? Is it provided by the details of his life or by the work he has created? Can he be said to have two biographies? Or one only that feeds on both these sources? Wherever one chooses to place the greatest emphasis, the fact remains in the case of Isaac Babel that the relationship between his life and his work is for a biographer, indeed for anyone trying to understand the man and evaluate the artist, of quite crucial importance.

Most of Babel's stories are told in the first person. To see the "I" of these stories as being absolutely identical with the author himself would be unforgivably naive. It is only too easy to demonstrate how often details in the life of Babel's narrator differ from those in Babel's own life. Such divergences should not, nevertheless, be allowed to obscure the vital point that the "I" of the stories of childhood and civil war has much in common with Babel, both as regards the circumstances in which they find themselves and especially as regards their outlook on life.

The autobiographical element in most of Babel's work is very strong, but complicated by his habit of telescoping, omitting, and distorting facts relating to himself. While this is the prerogative of the imaginative writer and can be said indeed of almost any writer drawing on autobiographical material, it is also symptomatic of Babel's enigmatic personality. As a man he has always proved elusive, whether to those who knew him or to those who tried to write about him. A would-be biographer is confronted with the task of distinguishing fact from semifact or from complete fantasy, a task difficult enough at any time but made more so in the present instance, for Babel was a secretive man who loved to perplex. Any of his utterances purporting to be statements of fact have always to be treated with the utmost care.

The idea of confusing literary critics would have appealed greatly to Babel's sense of humor, as he had a poor opinion of the species and prided himself on being impervious to criticism, good or bad. The critic trying to discern the essential Babel in his writings must cope with an irony as formidable as any to be found in Russian literature. On this subject Babel's friend and fellow writer Konstantin Paustovsky has commented:

In the shrill sound of his voice was heard a persistent irony. Many people could not look into Babel's burning eyes. By nature Babel was a debunker. He liked to get people in a corner and was therefore regarded in Odessa as a difficult and dangerous man.

Without doubt Babel is "a difficult man" to pin down. To a large extent the reason for this lies in his love of storytelling. He was a true adult successor of the child whose life is narrated as follows in the story "In the Basement" (1930):

I was an untruthful boy. This came about from my reading. My imagination was always inflamed. One day I noticed a book about Spinoza in the hands of our top pupil Mark Borgman. He had just read it and could not wait to tell the boys round about him of the Spanish Inquisition. What he said was just a learned mumble. Borgman's words lacked poetry. I could not resist intervening. To those who wanted to listen to me I told of old Amsterdam, of the darkness of the ghetto, of the philosophers who cut diamonds. I added a lot of my own to what I had read in books. . . . My classmates gaped as they listened to this fantastic tale. It was told with enthusiasm. Unwillingly we split up when the bell rang.

The preceding extract indicates Babel's own attitude to facts, and the relation between those facts and the particular work that they inspired him to write. Paustov-

sky bears witness that, like the "untruthful boy," Babel
possessed a remarkable gift for imaginative verbal narra-
tion: "He was a storyteller of genius. His oral tales were
more powerful and more perfect than his written ones."
In common with the great nineteenth-century writer
Nikolay Gogol (like Babel a Ukrainian by birth) and
the brilliant Soviet short-story writer Mikhail Zoshchenko
(also of Ukrainian origin), Babel created stories that
lend themselves to being read aloud.

"My First Literary Fee," one of Babel's lesser-
known stories, written between 1922 and 1928, tells of a
young man of twenty who draws on his powers of inven-
tion in order to save face. This narrator goes to bed with
an experienced Georgian prostitute and, ashamed of his
complete lack of sexual knowledge, thinks up a barely
credible explanation. The gist of his entirely false story
is that, living for several years in homosexual relations
with older men, he has never been allowed to consort
with women. The prostitute believes him, generously
imparts to him the secrets of her profession, and refuses
next morning to take the sum of money negotiated the
night before, because she regards her client as a "little
sister." The two five-rouble pieces the narrator receives
back are "the first literary fee" of the story's title.

"A well-devised story need not try to be like real life.
Real life is only too eager to resemble a well-devised
story." In this way the young narrator of "My First
Literary Fee" explains why he made no great attempt to
render a credible account of his prior misfortunes. For
all his narrative skill, Babel found immense difficulty in
inventing plots and considered himself in this respect de-
ficient of imagination. Once, however, he had a base
upon which to build, he was comparatively satisfied. The
events of his life gave him such a base, gave him a fundamental truth that he could embroider, a reality that he
could enlarge or diminish in his own individual manner.

2

*A Jewish
Childhood*

Babel is among those writers whose work continues to be significantly influenced by upbringing and early environment, whether or not they intend it to be so. The date of his birth, unlike the date of his death, is in no doubt. The oldest child and only son of Jewish parents, he was born 13 July 1894 in the famous Black Sea port of Odessa. The autobiography that Babel prepared for publication in 1926 suggests that it was here he spent his entire childhood. This is, however, an example of his somewhat cavalier attitude toward facts, for, not long after the birth of their son, the Babels moved to nearby Nikolayev, another Black Sea port, where their only other child, Meri, was born in 1899. Not until 1905 did they return to Odessa.

Babel's links with Odessa never ceased to afford him deep enjoyment and satisfaction. He always seemed happier in his native city than anywhere else, claiming, for example, that he could write ten times better there than in Moscow. Odessa itself provides a key to the understanding of Babel's character. During his childhood it was perhaps the most cosmopolitan city in the Russian empire, containing colonies of people from both western and eastern Europe—English, French, Germans, Greeks, Albanians, Bulgarians, Poles, and Romanians, to name only some. The cosmopolitan nature of the city was further enhanced by the coming and going of foreign sailors. Babel himself wrote: "In Odessa there is a port, and in the port are steamers arrived from Newcastle, Cardiff, Marseilles, and Port Said. There are Negroes, Englishmen, and Americans." He once referred to Odessa as "our Marseilles," a city he took the opportunity to visit on his first trip to western Europe in the autumn of 1927. It was the Parisians, however, rather than the inhabitants of Marseilles, who reminded him of his fellow Odessites: " . . . the same unimpressive-looking, sharp-witted, self-confident kind of people." From the accounts of Babel and his contemporaries Odessa emerges as a city of multifarious character, offering unusual stimulation to the sensitive eye and ear. During the twentieth century, indeed, it has produced some outstanding writers in addition to Babel: the poet Edward Bagritsky; the celebrated satirical duo of Il'f and Petrov; and the novelist Valentin Katayev, who is writing to the present day.

Apart from Odessa itself, the most important factor in Babel's development was his Jewish birth. In the quarter of a century immediately preceding the Russian Revolution of 1917 the number of Jews in Odessa increased from 32.9% to 50% of the population. They tended to live together, and the Jewish part of the city, called the Moldavanka, was where Babel was born and later grew up after his family's decision to return to Odessa in 1905. (Babel was highly amused when the first English translation of his work referred to his mother as a *Moldavian* Jewess—that is, from Moldavia.) Babel wrote of the Moldavanka: "In Odessa there is a very poor, numerous, and suffering Jewish ghetto. . . ." In the strictest sense of the word, however, the Moldavanka was not a ghetto, and in Babel's time Jews were not legally confined to any particular quarter. But this suburb of Odessa, fairly or unfairly, had a notorious reputation. According to Paustovsky, for example, two thousand criminals, petty and violent, resided there. Moreover, in his stories and in his play set in the area, Babel emphasized its lawlessness and depicts its inhabitants as luridly and exotically as possible.

Babel's own family, however, seems to have been impeccably law-abiding and his father, Emmanuel, held the blameless post of sales representative for a firm of agricultural engineers. This respected patriarch, while ob-

serving the most important religious holidays, did not
bring up his son too severely in the Jewish faith. The
fact of the Babels' Jewish blood remained, nevertheless,
and they suffered accordingly. Anti-Jewish demonstra-
tions were always liable to break out, and fearful pogroms
occurred in 1905, the dress rehearsal for 1917. The immediate cause of hostility directed against the Jews was the
imperial manifesto of October 1905. This accorded them
certain civic rights and fanned into violence a resentment
that was never far below the surface and that such anti-
Semitic organizations as the Black Hundreds were not
slow to exploit. In two of his finest works, "The Story
of My Dovecote" and "First Love," both published in
1925, Babel poignantly describes a pogrom as seen
through the eyes of a partially comprehending child. Toward the end of "First Love" the terrifying events he has
witnessed begin to take their toll on the nervous system
of the boy narrator: "Thus began my illness. I was then
ten years old. The next morning I was taken to see a
doctor. The pogrom continued, but nobody touched us.
The doctor, a fat man, found that I had a nervous illness."
The gist of this information can confidently be taken to
apply to Babel himself. In March 1928 he wrote from
Paris to I. Livshits, a close friend in Odessa: "What I
am going through must be called by its proper name—it
is an illness, neurasthenia, like the one in the days of my
youth. . . ."

But the illness brought on by the pogroms in the
south of the Russian empire was not just physical. In 1905
the ten-year-old Babel became fully aware for the first time
of what it meant to be a Jew and of how his ethnic
origins set him apart from men of different race. The
illness from which he suffered was also of a racial nature
and afflicted him throughout his life. Paustovsky reports
how in the early 1920s Babel, his hands shaking, talked of

anti-Semitism and confessed complete ignorance of the reasons for it. Moreover, Babel's stories of childhood testify explicitly and implicitly to the unhappiness of the family of the boy narrator. In "The Story of My Dovecote" the narrator's mother "looked at me with a bitter pity, as though at a cripple, for she alone knew how unhappy our family was. All our male relatives were trusting toward other people and unwisely hasty in their actions, so that we never had any luck." Glancing back at his early years, the narrator of "Karl-Yankel" (1931) concludes the story of a dispute involving a Jewish baby boy with the words: " 'It is impossible,' I whispered to myself, 'that you won't be happy, Karl-Yankel. . . . It is impossible that you won't be happier than I was.' "

The Jewish community among which Babel grew up found itself subject to discrimination by the non-Jewish populace, many of whom feared the growing numbers and increasing privileges of this seemingly alien element. Discrimination was felt most keenly by the young Babel in the field of education. A non-Jewish schoolboy was invariably given preference over a Jewish boy of similar ability. Many of Babel's teachers showed open prejudice in their treatment of Jewish pupils, and only a very small proportion of the latter was allowed to progress to higher educational establishments.

In the early part of 1905 Babel was admitted to the Nicholas I Commercial School of Odessa, where he spent the following six years. He lived at first with two aunts and his maternal grandmother until, later in 1905, his parents moved from Nikolayev and were able to obtain accommodation of their own.

Emmanuel Babel possessed grandiose ambitions for his son and made him study such long hours at home that the boy came to look on school as a comparative place of rest. The future writer was short, bespectacled, and

weak-chested, with a passion for reading and an aversion
to music. Unfortunately for him, Jewish Odessa prided
itself on producing infant prodigies for the concert hall
(Misha El'man and Yasha Heifetz among them), and
fond fathers were wont to regard their sons as potential
musical geniuses. Babel's acquaintance with the violin
brought him untold anguish, as he had no talent whatso-
ever for the instrument. He seems to have shared the
attitude of the boy narrator in "Awakening" (1931), who
fiddled tunelessly away while studying the novels of
Turgenev or Dumas instead of the musical score. Babel's
love of reading tended to make him something of a
solitary, like the narrator of "In the Basement" (1931):
"I used to read during lessons, during the break, on the
way home, at night beneath the table, under cover of the
tablecloth that hung down to the floor. . . . I had no
friends. Who would have wanted to spend time with some-
one like that?" From an early age Babel was sacrificing
the opportunity for personal relationships to his love of
literature, as he was to do later when he was himself a
writer of repute.

In "Awakening" Babel examined the motives of Jewish fathers in Odessa who forced their children to practice
music. The main reason, he concluded, was that dreams
of the spectacular achievements of their offspring in the
future compensated for indignities and deprivations in the
present. Furthermore, in "The Story of My Dovecote"
the narrator refers to his father's "pauper pride and in-
comprehensible faith in our family becoming one day
richer and more powerful than anyone else on earth."
Babel's own father, though he knew hard times, was ma-
terially better off than the father in the childhood stories.
After the revolution, however, Babel appears to have
thought it wise to claim for his family more straitened
circumstances than had in fact obtained. His brief auto-

biography of 1926 is interpreted by his daughter Nathalie as an example of "Babel's intention . . . to present an appropriate past for a young Soviet writer who was not a member of the Communist party. . . ."

Babel's great gift as a schoolboy lay in the field not of music but of languages. Such was his fluency in French that at the age of fifteen he began to attempt stories in that language. Educational discrimination prevented him from entering the University of Odessa, after he left school in 1911, because of the numerical restrictions placed upon the acceptance of Jewish students. Consequently he was despatched to the Ukrainian capital of Kiev to continue his education at the Institute of Financial and Business Studies. At about this time Babel became interested in the ideas of Leo Tolstoy and steeped himself in the works of the great Russian writer who had died only in 1910. It is perfectly understandable that a sensitive, bookish young Jew of precarious health, who had seen so much violence and encountered so much racial hatred, should have been drawn to Tolstoyism with its emphasis on the brotherhood of man and nonresistance to evil. Babel's year-long absorption with the writings of Tolstoy may be viewed as an attempt to come to terms with his past. Eventually he was to do this by becoming a writer himself. Even when he did not draw directly for material upon these early experiences, they largely shaped the attitude he adopted in his stories.

3

A Literary Apprenticeship (1913-1922)

The earliest of Babel's known works, the story "Old Shloyme," first appeared in Kiev in February 1913. The theme is anti-Semitism, with members of a Jewish family being forced either to renounce their religion or be driven from their home. Daringly, the main focus chosen by the eighteen-year-old Babel is the deteriorated mind of a Jew of eighty-six.

The gauntness of the young Babel's style in this story reflects the cheerlessness of events. He tended, however, to indulge in more elaborate syntax than was later his wont, and there is no sign yet of the breathtaking image that was to become his stock-in-trade. In one other respect, too, the story differs from most of what was to follow. Babel's compassion for Shloyme remains clear and unequivocal throughout, even though the character is initially presented as an almost subhuman geriatric, forgotten by practically everyone and living only for his stomach. His later grief at the family's impending change of faith serves to humanize him and to make his eventual suicide more affecting than might have otherwise been the case. For a writer so young and inexperienced, "Old Shloyme" is a curious but not unimpressive beginning to a singular career.

The outbreak of World War I caused the Institute of Financial and Business Studies to be moved from Kiev to Saratov. It was here that another of the earliest extant examples of Babel's work, dated 12 November 1915, came to be written. This largely autobiographical sketch entitled "Childhood" and subtitled "At Grandmother's" has only recently appeared in print and tells in three or four pages of how the narrator spent with his paternal grandmother one Saturday that was typical of many. The piece provides few new facts (it was at his grandmother's that Babel used to undergo the torment of lessons from a music teacher). It does, however, give a brief but fascinating characterization of its subject, described by Nathalie Babel as "a rather formidable and wicked old lady with a great passion for her grandson." The grandmother in Babel's sketch emerges as an embittered, crotchety woman, caring only for her son, grandson, dog, and flowers, perpetually quarreling with the servants, reminiscing about the past and offering the narrator what she considered to be sound advice:

Study and you will get everything—riches and fame. You must know everything. Everyone will fall and humble themselves before you. You must be envied by everyone. Don't trust people. Don't have friends. Don't give them money. Don't give them your heart.

The most impressive features of this early work are the observant detachment of the writer from his subject and the detail selected to convey economically but forcefully the quintessential atmosphere of his grandmother's way of life. The sketch is valuable to the student of Babel because it points a direction in which his talent might have moved, if he had chosen—namely, toward psychological realism as an end in itself.

After graduating from the Saratov Institute in 1915, Babel returned to Kiev, where his future wife lived with her family, and then made his first trip to Leningrad (called Petersburg until 1914, and Petrograd from 1914 to 1924). His activities bring to mind, not for the last time, those of another Ukrainian-born, hopeful writer, Nikolay Gogol, who had come to seek fame and fortune in the great city nearly ninety years before. Ostensibly Babel went to Leningrad to study, but his main ambition seems to have been purely literary, for he hawked his stories round the editorial offices, only to be shown the door.

A turning point in Babel's career was his first meeting with the celebrated Russian writer Maxim Gorky in late 1916. It is a debatable question whether Gorky's most important contribution to Russian literature lay in what he wrote himself or in the influence he exerted on other writers and on behalf of writers whose talent he admired and whose interests he took to heart. His own literary output was enormous, though of extremely variable quality. Yet he always seemed to have time to help and encourage promising young writers, and after the revolution his efforts in support of not just writers, but of artists in general, who had incurred the displeasure of the politicians, were especially admirable. It was due to the good offices of Gorky that Babel made a modest début as a writer, for in November 1916 two of his stories appeared in Gorky's journal *Letopis'*.

Despite their immaturity these first stories are unmistakably in the style of the writer who achieved such renown in the mid-1920s. "Mama, Rimma, and Alla," however, promises more than it fulfills. The core of the story is conflict between different generations—in this case between a mother and her teenage daughters. In the absence of her husband, Varvara Stepanovna is having a trying time with the lodgers whom material circumstances compel her to keep. Moreover, both daughters are giving cause for concern. The elder, Rimma, is interested in a Polish student lodger—though not sufficiently to lose her virginity to him—and wants to leave home. The younger, Alla, believes she is pregnant and is caught by her mother about to take a boiling bath with a view to resolving the situation. The story ends somewhat lamely with Varvara writing a worried letter to her husband, who is a circuit judge, pouring out her troubles to him and wishing he were home to be a father to his children. This ending adds pathos to what has gone before, but minor domestic crises were not an ideal vehicle for Babel's literary talents.

"Il'ya Isaakovich and Margarita Prokof'yevna," the second of the two stories published in *Letopis'*, reveals a more assured touch. Very short, like many of Babel's stories, it is also extremely elliptical as regards the basic facts of the situation. Il'ya Isaakovich has come to Oryol from Odessa on business. For some unspecified reason the police order him to leave by the first train, threatening to eject him forcibly if he does not. Il'ya's business matters, also unspecified, make him reluctant to comply, and, when approached by a prostitute, Margarita, he is glad to be taken back to her room. He denies being a Jew, when she asks him outright, although his name suggests strongly that he is. Here most certainly lies the clue as to why the police want to get rid of him. Further elucidation is supplied by Babel's 1926 autobiography, in which he tells of arriving in Leningrad without a permit and having to avoid the law. No doubt Il'ya found himself in a similar position in Oryol. By staying with Margarita, however, he eliminates the need to stay at a hotel, which would be legally obliged to demand his passport and would thus learn of his nationality.

The appeal of the story lies in the relationship between prostitute and client that is developed laconically and mainly by means of dialogue. Nothing very much happens. After the first night the secretive Il'ya attends to his business, returning in the evening. He exchanges a few confidences with Margarita, writes some business letters, and prepares to leave by train the next morning without any fuss. Quite unexpectedly Margarita appears on the station platform bringing some pies for the journey, just as if she were a solicitous wife. She is clearly unhappy at Il'ya's going, but her words betray no emotion, and they part formally and politely with a handshake.

Though more concentrated, more unified, and better constructed than "Mama, Rimma, and Alla," "Il'ya Isa-

akovich" remains the work of a gifted beginner. Babel had
not yet achieved, on the one hand, a satisfactory balance
between spareness of form and on the other the kind of
detail that diverts and at the same time imparts the essence of a particular situation. Furthermore the comedy
and pathos are as yet overly muted. What both stories
signally lack is a factually dramatic background that can
serve as a base and against which the story can be set with
a resultant gain in perspective. Gorky's comment on
Babel's writing at this time was a shrewd one, as later
events were to show: "You know nothing . . . but guess
about a lot of things. . . . So go out and learn what life
is."

For all their deficiencies, these early stories reveal
two important facets of Babel's art. The first of these is
stylistic, or, to be more exact, syntactical. As a writer he
constantly strived for conciseness of expression and clarity
of line and tried to curb a verbal ebullience that attracted
him to ornate imagery. These strivings can best be appre-
ciated by a study of Babel's syntax. In "Il'ya Isaakovich,"
for example, there is no sentence longer than three lines.
With characteristic wit Babel told Paustovsky not to be
afraid of full stops: "Perhaps the sentences I write are
too short. Partly because of my everlasting asthma. I can't
speak for any length of time. I don't have enough breath
for that. The longer the sentences, the more severe my
asthma." In the story "Guy de Maupassant" (1932),
moreover, the narrator declares: "No iron can penetrate
the human heart with such stunning force as a full stop
put in the right place." Not all English translators have
remained faithful to the syntactical structure Babel built
up with such deliberation, and it is with a feeling of
unease that the critic commits himself to an involved sentence when writing of Babel and his work.

Rhythmic modulation was of vital concern to Babel

even in his earliest stories, and he devoted close attention to the use of the paragraph and of punctuation marks:

All paragraphs and all punctuation marks must be used correctly, but from the point of view of producing the maximum effect on the reader and not according to some dead rule book. The paragraph is a particularly wonderful thing. It allows one quietly to change the rhythm and often, like a flash of lightning, it reveals to us a familiar sight in an entirely unexpected form. There are good writers who yet distribute paragraphs and punctuation marks just anyhow. And so, for all the high quality of their prose, it looks muddled, written in haste, and careless.

The second important aspect of Babel's work exemplified by these early stories is his predilection for humor of a sexual nature—a predilection he shared with, among others, a great contemporary writer, Evgeny Zamyatin. The Russian literary watchdogs were, on Babel's own testimony, not amused. Apparently he would have been arraigned on a charge of pornography but for the timely overthrow of the czar in February 1917. Babel stated that the charge against him was also to have included blasphemy and sedition. As neither story seems to warrant such an accusation, one ought perhaps to accept Babel's evidence here with a pinch of salt, until more reliable proof is forthcoming.

At the end of 1916 and beginning of 1917 four works of a different kind appeared under the general heading *Leaves from My Notebook.* All are short, impressionistic pieces of journalism, and, to a greater or lesser extent, all deal with literature.

"The Public Library" presents Babel's individual view of the staff and readership at the famous library in Leningrad during World War I. Not for nothing does he allude to Gogol. People are perceived through a distorting lens, including a Jew, "a martyr to the book," who

may be said to embody in exaggerated form an aspect of
Babel himself. The whole scene is put in some perspective
with a closing reference to the war and to the blood flowing at that time in the Carpathians.

"The Nine" is a similar piece, the portraits here
being of the types who frequent the editorial offices of
literary magazines. Babel blended disturbingly cynicism
and sympathy as he describes the nine different categories,
which range from the hopelessly eccentric to the pitifully
unfortunate.

For a biographer "Odessa" is the most interesting
and informative of these sketches. It is typical of Babel's
irony that he should have begun a piece that extols his
birthplace: "Odessa is a very squalid city. Everyone
knows that. . . ." As well as presenting a very personal
view of Odessa, he also suggests that it may have a signifi-
cant contribution to make to Russian literature: ". . . the
fruitful, life-giving influence of the south, of Russian
Odessa, perhaps (who knows?) of the only city in Russia
that can produce that national Maupassant of whom we
stand in such need." The short stories of Maupassant
were for Babel models of the genre and provided a constant source of inspiration to him, especially during the
early part of his literary career.

In the last of these articles, "Inspiration," a young
hopeful reads to the narrator a completed story that proves
boring and without talent. The latter tries to suggest
gently that it needs further polishing but in the end cannot bring himself to be unkind and delivers a few words
of praise with the qualification that technique is lacking,
though this will eventually come. When the two friends
part, the narrator feels profoundly depressed. What had
first struck him about the manuscript was the absence of
any corrections. To Babel himself this would have been
unthinkable. In an article, "Work on a Short Story"

(1934), he tells a young writer: "I am particularly fond of rewriting. There are some people who write a thing and can't bear to look at it afterward. With me it's different: the first draft is difficult for me, but I like to rewrite." The number of different drafts Babel once made of a short story, "Lyubka the Cossack" (1924), astonished Paustovsky, who reports Babel as saying that ". . . between the first and last variants there can be as much difference as between greasy wrapping paper and Botticelli's *Spring*." Indeed, the apparent fluency of Babel's style was achieved only after painstaking reworking, which he described as "slave labor": "After every story I age a few years."

One further work, "Doudou," should be mentioned here, since it also appeared under the *Leaves from My Notebook* banner in March 1917. Unlike the four preceding pieces, "Doudou" is pure story, illustrating Babel's idiosyncratic taste for the erotic. The nurse and dancer, Doudou, is an uncomplicated example of feminine sexuality, whose warmth and spontaneity have patent appeal for the narrator. While calculated to shock the bourgeois, the love-making scene between Doudou and the legless and dying French pilot is yet dramatically essential and excruciatingly moving. (The narrator hovers ambiguously in the background as a silent witness.) "Doudou," written with devastating brevity and certainty of touch, remains one of the most technically accomplished among Babel's early stories, though, at the same time, it is one of the least known.

The years from 1917 to 1920 formed part of Babel's literary apprenticeship less because of work published, which was small, than because of experience of life accumulated. He may be regarded, in fact, as curiously fortunate that so soon after Gorky's advice to get out among people, Russia underwent violent and dramatic changes that, from the writer's angle, provided sufficient new material for many years to come.

In 1917 the residence permit allowing Jews to live in Leningrad was abolished. That October Babel volunteered for the Russian army and served at the Romanian front until the following year, when he was sent back to Odessa after falling ill with malaria. There was no need for Babel to have volunteered for the army, as he had been excused from military service in 1914, but his decision to do so may be interpreted as a determined attempt to follow Gorky's advice. After convalescence Babel, according to his own statement, served in Leningrad with the Cheka, the counterrevolutionary organ that was developed into the Russian political police force. Soviet commentators like to insist that he often referred with pride to his service, which is also mentioned in the largely autobiographical "The Journey" (1932), but denied by those members of his family who emigrated to western Europe. The summer of 1918 found him on the Volga requisitioning grain to feed the starving cities, an episode remembered in the story "The S. S. *Cow-Wheat*" (1932). Babel does not seem to have been sufficiently enamored of the revolution, however, to join the Communist party, and there is no evidence that he ever did so.

An insight into Babel's original attitude toward the revolution is provided by several journalistic pieces of 1918. Published by Gorky in his newspaper *Novaya zhizn'*, they appeared under the general title of *Diary*.

It is characteristic of Babel, that, in depicting post-revolutionary life, he should have concentrated mainly on fringe matters rather than central issues. This is not the case, however, in "Mosaic," where the subject is religion. The strength of the religious feeling encountered by the Bolsheviks is not played down. One antireligious speaker has his meeting disrupted by irate members of the public.

Moreover the final impression left is of greater numbers than ever attending church in search of solace during the troubled days shortly after the October Revolution.

An outspoken attack against the People's Commissariat for Welfare is contained in "A Fine Institution." Here Babel described a home for juvenile delinquents and finds the staff unqualified, dishonest, and immoral and the children largely illiterate and underfed. In "The Blind Men" he concentrated on a more unusual institution—for blind war veterans—and examined the unsatisfactory situation of them and their families.

"Evacuees" is a bitterly ironic piece. In the unjust days before the revolution, wrote Babel, the factories were working. Now, in the days of justice, they have ceased production and the workers are driven from pillar to post. Three families who try to leave for home on a poorly made raft are drowned in the Neva, and the state that had seemed to care so little for their well-being when they were alive proceeds to treat them generously now they are dead.

While "Premature Babies" and "The Palace of Motherhood" would appear to have much in common, Babel's tone in each is very different. In the first he showed the plight of wet nurses expected to feed four premature babies as well as their own but who receive only three-eighths of a pound of bread per day. Looking ahead to the future, Babel feared that, if the babies survive at all, they will enjoy only three-eighths of a life. "The Palace of Motherhood," by contrast, is more complimentary to the new regime. A czarist school for well-to-do orphans had been converted into a home where expectant mothers will be cared for and educated in their responsibilities. Babel's attitude here is one of enthusiastic approval: "We must ensure that children are born properly. That is true revolution—of that I am quite certain."

In "Evening" Babel described strolling through the Leningrad of 1918, juxtaposing accounts of the police beating of a puny seventeen-year-old suspect, the youth and gaiety of German soldiers at a cafe a few streets away, and the charm of the city at a time when the white nights are beginning. "I shall not draw conclusions. I don't feel like doing that," is how Babel introduced his story. Though this may be seen as a trifle disingenuous, Babel did refrain from explicit judgments, conveying implicitly the violence, gaiety, and beauty that he discerned as making up the warp and woof of the revolutionary time.

"The Beast Is Silent," also set in Leningrad, examines the effect of the food shortage on caged animals. In the first of its two parts, Babel described a visit to the zoo, paying most attention to an old and starving ape and the crowd watching it. There is a typically shocking incident: "The ape had abandoned itself to a vile occupation. Thus dim-witted old men amuse themselves in the villages, as do little boys who hide behind piles of rubbish in a backyard." An erotic element is introduced when a soldier seems to make a pick-up in front of the ape's cage, but this is merely light relief, and the emphasis remains on the suffering of animals who cannot speak for themselves.

The second part tells of the arrival of a gray-bearded commission at the zoo to decide which animals are most dispensable: "The elephant, pacing about restlessly on high ground, kept stretching out and then curling up its trunk, but received no food." In a very poignant and skillful way Babel thus commented on the tribulations of Leningrad's human population by referring to the hunger of its captive animals.

Rather less successful is the piece entitled "Finns." A detachment from the far north, recruited against the Germans by the hard-pressed Reds, is described at an

otherwise deserted Finnish railway station. The bleakness
of the scene is matched by the quality of Babel's prose, as
he depicted men who have little chance of survival in face
of the Teutonic military machine. Babel's understatement,
however, appears here to have been misjudged, for the
piece is suffused with an unrelieved dullness and vague-
ness, so that the feelings of the reader are barely engaged.

As its title suggests, "An Incident on Nevsky" returns us to Leningrad. The focus this time is on a one-
armed young ex-prisoner-of-war who, faint with hunger,
collapses in the street. Passers-by are moved by his plight
and treat him generously, but the final picture is of the
cripple himself, as he fidgets on the asphalt and lets out
peals of laughter that are both "happy and meaningless."

The journal in which these pieces first appeared was
closed down in late 1918 and significantly they have not
been published since in the Soviet Union. In his postrevolutionary *Diary* Babel is shown not only as a stylist of
unusual promise but also as a compassionate observer concerned with the underprivileged and disabled, suffering
under a régime that never ceases to proclaim its humanity.

The only story by Babel known to have been published in 1918 was the slight anecdote entitled "Shabos-
Nahamu," the name of a Jewish holiday. The hero is a
comic Jew, Gershele, of whom the reader is told: "Not
for nothing had his fame spread throughout all Astropol,
all Berdichev, and all Vilyuysk." This remark, taken together with the way the story was presented as being
"from the cycle *Gershele*," suggests the existence of other
works about the same character, but none have so far been
discovered and, quite possibly, none were ever written.
In context the story resembles a folk tale with the crafty
hero outwitting a simple-minded innkeeper and his wife in
order to feed himself and a starving family. In style,
however, it differs little from the stories of 1916, except

that the language is more witty and the imagery more ambitious. The description of the innkeeper's wife, for instance, contains a simile of the kind for which Babel became noted: "Her high breast resembled two small sacks crammed full of grain."

In the winter of 1918–19 Babel was working for the People's Commissariat for Education (Narkompros) and later in 1919 returned to Odessa to marry Evgeniya (Zhenya) Gronfeyn, whom he had first met during his student days in Kiev. According to Paustovsky, Zhenya's parents objected to the match so vehemently that the young couple had to elope and Zhenya forfeited her inheritance. According to Babel's sister, the elopement story told to Paustovsky by Babel was not true and merely a jocular figment of her brother's imagination.

The main interest shared by Babel and his wife was a passion for the arts. Zhenya is described by those who knew her as having been an artist of genuine talent. The Russian émigré, Yury Annenkov, pictures her in his memoirs as a very cultured woman weighed down by family matters. The well-known writer, Il'ya Erenburg, one of the few prominent Jews to survive under Stalin, is less kind and more class conscious in his autobiography: "Babel's first wife, Evgeniya Borisovna, grew up in a bourgeois family, and it was far from easy for her to get used to the whims of Isaac Emmanuilovich." Paustovsky says surprisingly little about her other than that she was "a redheaded beauty."

Babel's service on the Romanian front had not apparently satisfied his appetite for military life. In 1919 he became attached to the Northern Army, which prevented anti-Bolshevik troops led by General Yudenich from seizing Leningrad. The following year he joined the ranks of the First Cavalry Army under the command of Budyonny, which drove the Poles out of the Ukraine and pursued them into their own country in the hope of total victory. Out of this last experience grew Babel's most famous work, *Konarmiya* (literally *Horse Army*, but usually translated, and referred to hereafter in this book, as *Red Cavalry*). During the campaign he acted as war correspondent for ROSTA, the news agency of the new Soviet Union. Reports of his death proved, as in the celebrated case of Mark Twain, to have been false, and at the end of the year he returned to Odessa in poor physical shape, covered in vermin, and suffering acutely from asthma.

Babel's concern with war at this juncture is conveyed by four stories published in an Odessan journal in 1920 and set during the 1914–18 campaign. Somewhat surprisingly he did not draw directly on his own military experiences, and three of the stories are based on the memoirs of a French officer.

"On the Field of Honor" and "The Deserter" both examine the fear of a common soldier. In the former a country simpleton is goaded into action only after he has been urinated on. Charging wildly forward he is shot first by the enemy and then by his own officer. The twenty-year-old deserter in the second story is given an opportunity to choose suicide instead of court martial. Unable to press the trigger, however, he, too, is shot by a French officer. Most horrifying of all is "The Family of Old Marescot." The graveyard setting and the details of devastation with corpses spilling out of their coffins obviously appealed to Babel's sense of the macabre. So must have the idea of the old peasant bringing to the family crypt in a sack the remains of his wife and children.

Finally, "The Quaker" tells of a man killed as the direct consequence of his love for a horse. This is the only one of the four stories not based on a French original. The hostility between the Quaker and a stableboy lends it

greater complexity, and it benefits also from a diminu-
tion of Babel's desire to shock, which is all too evident
in the other stories. Inevitably, the Quaker's isolation,
pacifism, and attachment to horseflesh bring to mind
Lyutov, the narrator of *Red Cavalry*.

It was in 1921 that Paustovsky met Babel in
Odessa and that Babel's story, "The King," appeared in
an Odessan journal. The first of Babel's tales about his
native Moldavanka convinced Paustovsky "that another
wizard had entered our literature and that nothing written
by this man would ever lack life or color."

In "The King" Babel made no effort to achieve
psychological realism by means of detached observation
and carefully selected detail as in the portrait of his grandmother. In the Moldavanka stories he preferred grotesque
representation, the depiction of larger-than-life characters,
and the colorfulness of his prose does not pale by comparison with the raspberry waistcoats of the "aristocrats
of the Moldavanka" and the orange suit of their "king,"
Benya Krik. Benya's genealogy may be traced back three
years to Gershele, hero of "Shabos-Nahamu." Both are
Jews who live by their wits and never seem lost for a
word or a way out of a tricky situation. But, whereas
Gershele is poor and impotent, Benya is rich, powerful,
and violent. An obsession with violence runs like a black
seam throughout Babel's work, and the Moldavanka stories are one of several attempts to come to terms with it
by means of exaggerated and even comic representation.
Instead of a gentle all-suffering King of the Jews, Babel
enshrined as his hero an incredibly ruthless and majestic
King of the Criminals. Babel's attitude toward Benya
appears to have been one of awe for his ability to exploit
the conditions of the Moldavanka and earn the respect
and fear of its inhabitants in a manner Babel himself
could never hope to emulate: "And he got his own way,
did Benya Krik, because he was passionate, and passion

can rule worlds." It is tempting to regard Benya, if not exactly as an example of wish fulfillment on Babel's part, then as an embodiment of those attributes of mind and body that were entirely alien to Babel and toward which he held an ambivalent attitude.

The central event in "The King" is the wedding feast of Benya Krik's ugly older sister, Dvoyra. Though worried that the new police chief intends to take advantage of the situation to round up those criminals present, Benya remains unperturbed. A flashback relates how he had extorted money from the rich Eykhbaum and ended up by becoming his son-in-law. Babel then returns the reader to the luxurious feast. The guests smell burning, which in fact comes from the blazing police station. Benya completes his triumph over "the new broom" by strolling down to the fire with two friends and offering condolences. The story ends, however, at the scene of the carousing and with a situation more spine chilling than the cutting of the throats of Eykhbaum's cows on the orders of Benya:

The guests went their ways, and the musicians dozed, leaning their heads on their double basses. Only Dvoyra had no thought of sleep. With both hands she was pushing her enervated husband toward the door of their nuptial chamber, looking at him carnivorously, like a cat, which, holding a mouse in its jaws, tries it carefully with its teeth.

The final sentence of the extract is unusually complicated, but affords an exquisitely grotesque example of Babel's sexual humor. Indeed, "The King" as a whole is characteristic of his best work, as the background is one that he knows intimately and that allows him to flex his stylistic muscles with complete confidence.

The Moldavanka milieu gave Babel the opportunity to develop his gift for bizarre contrast and juxtaposition. This quality is also much in evidence in "An Evening at the Empress's," which was published in 1922 as an extract from his *Petersburg Diary*. The narrator finds himself in Leningrad without shelter, and Babel likened his plight to his own painful musical experiences as a child: "Hunger was sawing at me, like an ungifted lad at the string of a violin." He decides to try his luck at the Anichkov Palace, former residence of the Empress Maria Fyodorovna, widow of Alexander III, and mother of Nicholas II, the last of the Romanovs. Grotesque contrasts between the poverty of the narrator and the opulence of his surroundings are expressed in taut and witty prose:

That evening I dined like a human being. I laid out on an engraved Chinese table, glittering with ancient varnish, the most delicate of serviettes. Every piece of that coarse ration of bread I washed down with tea, sweet, steaming, and playing with the coral stars on the faceted walls of the glass. The velvet of the seats stroked my skinny sides with their bloated palms.

The displacement of the old by the new in postrevolutionary Russia gave Babel ample scope for writing of this kind. Obviously, though, he did not think he had exploited the full potential of the situation described in "An Evening at the Empress's," and in "The Journey" he incorporated a revised version.

In 1922 Babel left Odessa with his wife to seek the health-giving mountain air of the Caucasus, first in Batumi and then in Tbilisi. This period saw him begin *Red Cavalry*, the work that was to propel him to overnight fame as unexpectedly as *Evenings at a Village near Dikan'ka* had done in the case of Gogol.

Babel's literary apprenticeship had come to an end. The emergent writer was to capitalize handsomely on the knowledge of life acquired during these years and to more than justify the hopes of Gorky, his mentor.

4

Red Cavalry

Stories from *Red Cavalry* began to be published as early as 1923, but Babel himself liked to date his literary career from 1924, when several stories in the sequence came out in the fourth number of the journal *LEF*. Two years later *Red Cavalry* appeared for the first time as a complete entity. It consisted of thirty-four stories (referred to usually as "novellas" by Russian critics), to which "Argamak" (dated 1924–30) was subsequently added.

To call the component parts of the work "stories" can be misleading. Some are almost entirely atmospheric ("The Cemetery in Kozin" and "Berestechko"). Many others record incidents seen and people met, in the manner of diary entries rather than stories. All are short. The longest covers no more than seven pages; the shortest less than one. *In toto*, nevertheless, *Red Cavalry* stands, both physically and aesthetically, as the most substantial of Babel's works.

Except when characters are allowed to speak for themselves, *Red Cavalry* is narrated in the first person by a certain Lyutov, about whose personal affairs information is only sparingly given. Like Babel, he is a be-spectacled Jewish unbeliever and a war correspondent who contributes to the cavalry newspaper. Unlike Babel, he graduated in law at Petersburg University, his wife has left him, and he decides ultimately to transfer to the active forces.

The resemblances between narrator and author are incomparably more important in shaping the presentation of events than are the differences. The choice of name for the narrator, though seldom mentioned, carries signifi-cance. First, it suggests to a Russian-speaking reader the adjective for "ferocious, violent," a connotation that proves painfully ironic within the context of the work. Secondly, Babel used the name more than once as a *nom de plume*. In September 1920 he wrote a straightforward sketch, "Her Day," which praised the nurses tending the wounded soldiers and which appeared in the newspaper *Red Cavalryman* under the pseudonym of K. Lyutov. The name also occurs in connection with journalistic work carried out in Tbilisi. Moreover, I. Livshits claims that his friend Babel first entered Budyonny's cavalry as Kirill Vasil'yevich Lyutov.

Additionally, the Lyutov of *Red Cavalry* shares with his creator a natural hedonism. All Babel's friends seem to have been struck by his unashamed love of life: "Man lives for pleasure, to sleep with a woman, to eat an ice cream on a hot day." This remark, quoted with relish by Erenburg, harmonizes with the reasons for the friendship between Lyutov and the Cossack officer Khlebnikov: "We both looked at the world as at a May meadow through which pass women and horses" ("The Story of a Horse").

Khlebnikov is one of the rare friends Lyutov succeeds in making among the Cossack cavalrymen, and his dominant mood is rather that of depression: " 'Galin,' I said, overcome by pity and loneliness, 'I'm ill, my end seems to have come, and I am tired of living in our Cavalry . . .' " ("Evening"). For a long time he feels a pariah. His misery is increased when Khlebnikov leaves the army, and another of his friends, Afon'ka Bida, turns against him for refusing to put a fatally wounded man out of his agony: "You bastards with glasses have as much pity for blokes like us, as a cat for a tiny mouse . . ." ("The Death of Dolgushov"). This last episode spotlights one of the fundamental differences between Lyutov and the Cossacks—their attitude toward human life. Whereas there are many instances of cavalrymen killing without compunction, Lyutov cannot bring himself to do so even when, in the case of Dolgushov, this is the lesser of two evils. Only hunger seems to rouse him to violence. He is

quite prepared to shoot an old woman whom he believes
to be hiding food ("The Song"), and, in a similar situation, kills the goose of a reluctant landlady ("My First
Goose"), though later he feels that his heart has been
stained by murder.

Lyutov's horror at the apparently casual way Cossacks spill blood often brings him into conflict with
them. He protests at the shooting of unarmed prisoners
by the squadron commander Trunov and after the latter's
death is reproached by another soldier: ". . . you pick
quarrels with everyone. There's some devil sitting in you,
Lyutov" ("Squadron Commander Trunov"). In "After
the Battle" he is accused of riding into the fray without
cartridges in his revolver and later prays for the capacity
to kill—a startling stroke of irony. Finally, in "Argamak,"
a young squadron commander expresses contempt for
Lyutov's desire to live without enemies. Paradoxically he
does make enemies of the Cossacks and reflects in the
same story, the last of the sequence: "I was alone among
these people whose friendship I had failed to win."

Babel's solitariness both as a child and later as a
mature writer dedicated to his art, indicates the likelihood
of his having been something of a lone figure in the First
Cavalry Army. In common with Lyutov he was a well-
educated Jew, physically unimpressive, to whom any
Cossack cavalryman would have been the opposite in almost every way. The outward symbol of Lyutov's sepa-
rateness from the Cossacks is the eyeglasses that he wears
(as did Babel) and that make him a frequent butt for
insults: "A young chap with flaxen hair hanging down
and the handsome face of a Ryazan' Cossack went up to
my trunk and threw it out of the gate. Then he turned
his back on me and with singular skill began to emit
shameful sounds" ("My First Goose").

Not only did the Cossacks profess contempt for any kind of learning, but, moreover, the intellectual who had received his education under the czarist régime became an object of suspicion in Russia after the revolution of 1917. The postrevolutionary hero was usually the worker of impeccable proletarian origin in whose name the Bolsheviks had seized power, and there were many advocates of a new morality and culture created by such men who had not been contaminated by the old way of life. The intellectual who remained in postrevolutionary Russia—and many thousands emigrated to the West—had been contaminated and needed to prove his loyalty to the creed of the new government before he could win acceptance. His dilemma found reflection in Soviet literature to such an extent that the tortured intellectual, trying, with varying success, to come to terms with communism, emerged as a stock character, to whose ranks Pasternak's Dr. Zhivago can be seen to belong.

Lyutov's difficulties in Budyonny's First Cavalry Army are further complicated because he is a Jew, surrounded by Cossacks, the traditional enemies of his race. At the center, therefore, of *Red Cavalry*, Babel erected a monstrously incongruous situation, which lent itself happily to his literary gifts and proclivities. A further incongruity is that the Cossacks fight in the name of revolution, even though they are so benighted politically and for about two centuries had given formidable military support to the Russian autocracy. From the eighteenth century until the overthrow of Nicholas II, Cossacks played an active part in all Russia's external campaigns, and revolutionary hopes of 1905 were crushed largely by their sabers. In 1917 most of them opposed Lenin, fearing the loss of the land they received from the emperor in return for military services. Yet, despite their age-old traditions and prejudices, here they were only three years later serv-

ing revolutionary masters whose aims and ideals they
barely understood, let alone shared.

Well before Babel, three of Russia's most eminent
writers had been inspired to devote their artistic attentions
to the Cossacks. In *The Captain's Daughter* Pushkin
used as background the Pugachov revolt on the Yaik
river, which shook the autocracy during the early 1770s.
In "Taras Bul'ba" Gogol dealt in typically offhand historical fashion with the Zaporozh'ye Cossacks, forefathers
of the modern Ukrainians. Finally, in *The Cossacks*
Tolstoy chose as his heroes the Cossack community he
had encountered while on active military service in the
Caucasus. Like Babel, all three looked at the Cossack
from outside. On the other hand, the best and most
authentic work featuring the Cossacks is *The Quiet Don*
by Mikhail Sholokhov, a Don Cossack, who can view his
subjects from the inside and present them at peace as well
as at war. Pushkin, Gogol, Tolstoy, and Babel, however, showed the Cossack, for the most part, only as a
fighting man, and their admiration for his redoubtable
physical prowess tends to turn him into a distorted and
one-dimensional figure. Contrary to the historical evidence, Pushkin's Pugachov emerges as quite a gentle-
manly rebel, standing rather apart from the atrocities com-
mitted in his name and almost tragic in his powerlessness
to control events. Gogol's Taras Bul'ba is a titanic
caricature of incredible fortitude, while Tolstoy's Cau-
casian Cossacks are attractively spontaneous and extrovert in favorable contrast to the young Muscovite officer,
Olenin.

Because of his Jewish blood, Babel's view of the
Cossacks was more complex, more stark, less romantic
(though by no means devoid of romanticism), and suffused with an ambivalence not to be found in any of the
nineteenth-century authors just mentioned. The system of

values by which the Cossacks live is repugnant to Lyutov, and yet he cannot help admiring them. The young soldier Kurdyukov typically reveals the Cossack priorities when writing home. Not until he has inquired about the condition of his horse does he tell in childishly naive language about how his father was done to death by his sons in a brutal act of revenge ("The Letter").

Babel's own service with the cavalry instilled in him a deep love for horses; the loss of his horse was the worst punishment a Cossack could suffer ("Argamak"). When he loses his mount in battle, Lyutov's former best friend runs amok and butchers the Poles without mercy ("Afon'ka Bida"). Khlebnikov leaves the service because his horse has been wrongfully taken from him by another officer ("The Story of a Horse"). To Cossacks, horses seem to mean more than do human beings, and when Lyutov learns to ride in their style, they stop looking at him with such contempt. One is reminded of this latter instance by Babel's play *Sunset* (1928), when Benya Krik's hussar brother Lyovka declares: "A Jew who mounts a horse ceases to be a Jew and becomes a Russian."

Since *Red Cavalry* deals with war, no one should be surprised that its pages positively reek of blood. Much of it, however, is spilt gratuitously, even dispassionately, by the Cossacks. The eponymous hero of "Konkin" dispatches a Polish prisoner seemingly out of boredom, just because he cannot be bothered with him any longer. In "Berestechko" Kudrya coolly slits an old Jew's throat, and his main concern is not to splash himself with blood. Pavlichenko, in "The Biography of Pavlichenko, Matvey Rodionych," tells how he spent a whole hour trampling to death his former master. In all these men there is an essential element that Lyutov finds absent in himself and that he seeks to comprehend. He comes closest to a def-

inition when, after battle, he discerns in the newly pro-
moted Kolesnikov "the masterful indifference of the
Tartar khan" ("The Commander of the Second
Brigade").

In accordance with the preeminence of the working
man after the revolution, Budyonny's officers are mostly
of humble origin, Pavlichenko, for example, having been
a shepherd in civilian life. Moreover, the mortality rate
in the First Cavalry Army could lead to rapid promotion,
as in the case of Kolesnikov, in "The Commander of the
Second Brigade": "An hour ago Kolesnikov commanded
a regiment. A week ago Kolesnikov commanded a
squadron." The literacy of such men is poor, and their
understanding of the postrevolutionary situation, to say
the least, primitive. The politically conscious Galin believes, however, that with time the Cossacks will be correctly educated by the Communist party and will lose the
prejudices in which they are steeped ("Evening").

In several stories Babel let Cossacks tell a particular
story in their own words (a literary form known in
Russian literature as the *skaz*). Their ignorance thus
speaks for itself, and humorous verbal effects are created,
as when in "Salt" Balmashev attempts to use communist
jargon in describing how he shot a woman: "And I took
from the wall my trusty rifle and wiped this disgrace
from the face of the workers' land and republic." The
Cossacks are unabashed at their lack of even elementary
learning, despising the "four-eyes" in their midst. Only
when Lyutov proudly reads aloud a speech by Lenin from
Pravda, does his literacy impress them at all favorably
("My First Goose").

Babel's depiction of the Cossacks must be seen as part
of his general attitude toward violence, which he found
simultaneously repellent and fascinating. In this respect
there is a marked similarity between him and the Don

Cossack, Sholokhov, whose work is also filled with gruesome detail and who lingers almost lovingly on scenes of
violent death. In the third volume of *The Quiet Don*,
for example, it is physically painful to read how Red
Cossack prisoners are slowly hacked to pieces by the inhabitants of the villages through which they pass, and one
could quote numerous other harrowing passages. Two instances of gruesome tendencies on Babel's part occur
when, in "The Ivans," Lyutov finds himself urinating on
a corpse in the darkness, and when pieces of the brain of a
prisoner, whose head has been shot off, drip over Lyutov's
hands in "Squadron Commander Trunov." *Red Cavalry*
stands as eloquent testimony of what Lionel Trilling refers to in an essay on Babel as "the powerful and obsessive
significance that violence has for the intellectual."

Another common bond between Babel and Sholokhov is their overwhelming feeling for the physical
strength and animal attractiveness of the Cossack male.
In "My First Goose," for example, Lyutov is lost in admiration for the sheer bodily beauty of Savitsky, commander of the Sixth Division, and communicates it
through references to women: "He smelled of scent and
the sickly freshness of soap. His long legs were like girls,
sheathed up to the shoulders in gleaming riding boots."
The physical impression left by these lines is so intense
that it seems almost as though Savitsky and the Jewish
narrator belong not only to different milieus but to different sexes as well.

An important point is that the Cossacks are shown
abhorring Lyutov as an intellectual but not as a Jew, presumably because they do not know he is one. (Trilling
suggests Babel may have made this omission out of fear
for the political censorship.) The poignant situation of a
Jew participating in Budyonny's campaign is rendered in
other ways. Sometimes these are unemphatic, as when

Lyutov, in "My First Goose," eats pork with the other soldiers, and incidental, as when in "Zamost'ye" a Polish peasant tells Lyutov, not knowing who he is, that the Jews are to blame for everything. But the main circumstance that reminds Lyutov of his origins is his constant contact with the Polish Jews, most of whom drag out a squalid existence in their villages.

The religious position of Lyutov seems to have been identical with that of Babel himself, who professed to be an atheist (though his sister denies this). He took particular pleasure in the kind of writing a Christian would consider blasphemous and was not averse to mocking Judaism either. In *Red Cavalry* a hero of Lyutov's is Apolek, the painter who offends the village priest by using local inhabitants to represent biblical characters in his church murals: "The wise and wonderful life of Apolek went to my head like old wine" ("Pan Apolek"). Apolek also amuses Lyutov by recounting an indecent story about Christ, and Lyutov later returns home "warming within me unfulfillable dreams and wild songs." It is characteristic of Babel's irony that the gentle Cossack, Sashka, nicknamed "Christ," should be a syphilitic who dispenses comfort to unhappy women ("Sashka the Christ"). Examples are given also of the Cossacks' crude humor directed against religious belief, as when Savitsky writes of rumors that "the old chap in Heaven has not a kingdom but a regular brothel."

In family correspondence, as well as in his stories, Babel could be blasphemous. Writing to his mother and sister in April 1928 he referred to "that old crook, the Jewish God." Perhaps, however, he protested too much, and, when his much-loved mother fell ill, we find him claiming in October 1935: "In Odessa I have rediscovered the existence of God and pray to him for Mama's recovery." While one always has to make allowances for

Babel's habitual tongue-in-cheek attitude, irony at such a time would seem to have been out of place.

Despite his rational rejection of religion, Lyutov is unable to escape the influences of the Jewish faith in which he was nurtured. "Gedali," for example, begins with an admission of the sad memories that overcome him each Sabbath eve. This moving story pivots upon an argument between Lyutov and an old Jew, Gedali, who keeps a "curiosity shop." Lyutov speaks as an advocate of the Bolshevik Revolution, but Gedali asks whether saying "yes" to it must mean saying "no" to the Sabbath. Gedali confesses difficulty in distinguishing between revolution and antirevolution, when both employ the same sanguinary methods, and dreams of "an International of good people." His attitude typifies that which Lyutov and Babel were brought up to adopt, and this side of the narrator is uppermost when he formally denounces those Cossacks who had caused an outrage in church and offended the religious feelings of the local people ("In Saint Valentine's Church"). In anything pertaining to religion he displays a fine sensitivity that is only partially disguised by his omnipresent irony: "In the kitchen I was greeted by Eliza, the Jesuit's housekeeper. She gave me tea the color of amber and spongecakes. Her sponges smelt of the crucifixion. Their ingredients were a cunning juice and the sweet-swelling passion of the Vatican" ("The Church at Novograd").

Lyutov provides such an engrossing narrative, not only because of his dramatically anomalous position vis-à-vis the Cossacks, but also because of his sense of history. The very first story, "Crossing the Zbruch," finds him traveling from Brest to Warsaw along a road he describes as "built on peasant bones by Nicholas I." In "Treatise on the *Tachanka*," he remarks of the machine-gun cart that became a "mobile and redoubtable means of warfare": "I feel the heat of many generations in those springs jolting now over the churned roads of Volynia." In Berestechko, moreover, he ponders the history of the locality, and fresh perspective is given by the unexpected discovery of a fragment of a letter written in French and dated 1820 ("Berestechko").

The feeling for the past with which Babel endowed his narrator gives scope for contrasts with the revolutionary present and hoped-for future in the grotesque style he so favored. Indeed, one forms the impression that the material content of *Red Cavalry*, absorbing as it is for its own sake, was deliberately selected to show off those literary devices that are Babel's trademark. The main contrasts are between the Jewish mind and the Cossack body; between the Russian Jew in the ranks of the invader who has lost his faith and the Polish Jew in the ranks of the invaded who has kept his; between a brash atheistic revolutionary present and a crumbling religious past; between Lyutov's humane principles and their relevance or otherwise to the situations in which he finds himself. The atmosphere of violent conflict suggested to Babel such incongruous juxtapositions as the portraits of Lenin and Maimonides lying side by side and Communist pamphlets with ancient Hebrew verses written in the margins ("The Rabbi's Son"). He omitted supplying any kind of moral perspective, and this neutrality brought from the famous Soviet literary critic, Viktor Shklovsky, the sardonic comment: "He speaks in the same tone of voice about the stars and about gonorrhea." It is entirely in keeping with the work as a whole that, in "Zamost'ye," the information that the Russians have lost the Polish campaign should be conveyed *sotto voce*.

Red Cavalry provides a treasure house not only of vividly realized conflicts, but also of daring similes comprised of seemingly disparate halves. Most of these are derived in part from nature: "The moon hung over the yard like a cheap earring" ("My First Goose"); "the earth lay like the back of a cat overgrown with the twinkling fur of wheat" ("The Road to Brody"); "a song gurgled like a stream running dry" ("Berestechko"); "crimson warts like a radish in May" ("In Saint Valentine's Church"); and, finally, blood runs from a wound "like rain from a haystack" ("Squadron Commander Trunov"). An erotic simile is a more polished variant of one already quoted from "Shabos-Nahamu": "And she went up to the divisional commander, bearing her bosom on her heels, a bosom that moved like an animal in a sack" ("The Story of a Horse"). In sum, the style of *Red Cavalry* shows that very individual combination of conciseness and richness of language that is promised in Babel's earlier stories and distinguishes all his best work.

The reaction of Budyonny himself to *Red Cavalry* was one of outrage that his men should have been so slandered. In two articles (1924 and 1928) he attacked Babel as a rearguard observer who had never seen proper action and did not know what he was talking about. Gorky replied in defense of his protégé, who seemed not at all worried by this controversy and confessed that Budyonny's outburst made him swell up with glee. With the passage of time he became dissatisfied with *Red Cavalry* and even expressed a dislike for it in 1930: "... just a second-rate horsey! But then, just try and understand readers." Few critics have agreed with this judgment, however, and neither has the Russian public, which orders all the copies of each new edition long before they have had time to appear on the market. Unpublished works by Babel continue to be "discovered" in the Soviet Union, but, for the moment, *Red Cavalry* remains indisputably the most important and most popular of all Babel's writings.

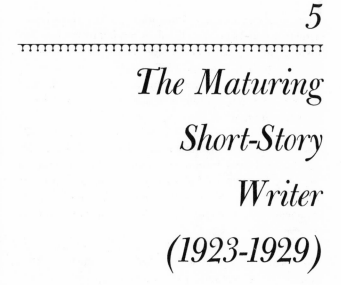

5

The Maturing

Short-Story

Writer

(1923-1929)

It is a matter of some frustration for the tidy-minded critic that Babel's creative life does not fall neatly into any obvious literary periods. By continuing to examine his work up to and through 1929, therefore, one is really doing little more than tracing his artistic development as far as a year that conveniently divides the remainder of his work into more or less equal halves.

The principal event of Babel's private life in 1923 was the death of his father in Odessa. Babel and his wife traveled there from the Caucasus at the beginning of the year. In 1924 he followed his mother and sister to Moscow where publication of some of the *Red Cavalry* sequence had aroused remarkable enthusiasm among readers.

Generally speaking, Babel's critics have tended to allow *Red Cavalry* to eclipse his other stories, which, with a few exceptions, have rated comparatively brief mention. The diversity of their subject matter is one reason for such neglect. Some are about childhood; others, in the style of "The King," about the Moldavanka. Some can be called erotic; others, from the Christian viewpoint, blasphemous. None of these categories, however, covers more than a handful of stories and certainly nothing at all comparable in quantity with the thirty-five stories that make up *Red Cavalry*. Furthermore, several stories cannot be classified together with any others. All, nevertheless, merit due critical consideration, and most of those published in the period 1923–29 reveal an increasingly confident technique, even though the effort required to achieve their very distinctive polish cost Babel no less dearly than before.

Of the stories published in 1923 and 1924 three are usually categorized together with "The King" as *Odessa Stories*. Two of these see the reappearance of Benya Krik. "How It Was Done in Odessa" recalls his early

days as a gangster before he had earned his regal sobri-
quet. The main story is told to a narrator by an old Jew,
Ar'ye-Leyb, as both sit on the wall of a cemetery. Benya
has joined the gang of Froim Grach (Froim the Rook),
another shady Moldavanka character, who puts his young
recruit to the test by entrusting him with the robbery of
one of the richest men in Odessa. During the operation a
blameless employee of this man is stupidly shot. By way
of recompense Benya arranges a funeral that is so sump-
tuous as to earn him the admiration of the whole of the
Moldavanka.

The tone of the story is very similar to that of "The
King" in its richness and humor. Benya, clad as extrava-
gantly as ever in chocolate jacket, cream trousers, and
raspberry boots, bestrides the action with colossal confidence and impertinence. In his demand note to the rich
Jew, Tartakovsky, he combines elaborate politeness with
threatening insolence. When the clerk is killed, Benya,
himself the indirect cause of the misfortune, demands
that Tartakovsky give generous compensation to the
bereaved mother and pay for the funeral, which is as
lavish an occasion as the wedding feast in "The King."
At the funeral, indeed, Benya makes a dramatic arrival
and delivers a magnificently hypocritical speech about the
deceased ("He perished for the whole working class").
Then he asks all those present to accompany to the grave
the drunken Jew who had shot the clerk in the first place
and who has now mysteriously expired!

As compared with "The King," "How It Was Done
in Odessa" gains extra perspective through being told
for the most part by Ar'ye-Leyb. The style he adopts is
an often comic medley of grave, quasi-biblical language
and subliterary Russian. The supposed dialogue of the
characters involved is quoted liberally for the benefit of
the overall narrator who, though rarely perceptible, is

compared to his disadvantage with the brilliantly successful Benya. This shy narrator, insofar as he is characterized
at all, seems physically inept (he never manages to get
the best seats on the cemetery wall) and is said by Ar'ye-
Leyb to have spectacles on his nose and autumn in his
soul. The reference to spectacles, so important in *Red
Cavalry*, suggests once again the timorous Jewish intellectual, this time fascinated by the Benya Kriks of the
Moldavanka whom he cannot hope to emulate and can
only wonder at from afar. At first he asks Ar'ye-Leyb to
tell him of Benya's "lightning beginning and terrible
end." In fact his terrible end is not told in this, or, as
far as one knows, in any other story.

Though Benya also appears in "The Father," main
attention is focused this time on the notorious Froim
Grach and his attempts at marrying off his Amazonian
daughter Bas'ka. The man for this mighty task proves to
be Benya Krik himself, once he has been persuaded to
leave a brothel run by a formidable lady known as Lyubka
the Cossack. (Presumably Babel had forgotten or could
not be bothered to remember that in "The King" he had
already married Benya to the daughter of the wealthy
Eykhbaum.)

It is in keeping with the expansive style of the
Moldavanka stories that Bas'ka should cut such an im-
posing figure ("She had vast sides and brick-colored
cheeks") and should dress so singularly: "She put on
men's boots, an orange dress, and a hat covered with
birds." It is also in keeping that Lyubka should know how
to use her fists, swear like a trooper, and be able to hold
her vodka. Both ladies would seem to be descendants of a
fierce Gogolian dame, the auntie who commands all the
manly qualities her timid nephew, Ivan Fyodorovich
Shpon'ka, so patently lacks ("Ivan Fyodorovich Shpon'ka
and His Auntie").

"Lyubka the Cossack" has as heroine the lady already introduced in "The Father." The subject of this amusing anecdote is how the little old Jew, Tsudechkis, came to be manager at Lyubka's establishment. At first he had been locked up after refusing to pay for services rendered. In the end, however, Lyubka has cause to be grateful to him. At a time when she cannot feed from the breast, Tsudechkis weans her baby son and, as a reward, is taken into her employment.

All three stories provide excellent examples of the Babel simile: "But meanwhile misfortune lurked under the windows like a beggar at dawn" ("How It Was Done in Odessa"); "The old man drank vodka from an enamel teapot and ate hash that smelled like a happy childhood" ("The Father"); "The sun drooped from the sky like the pink tongue of a thirsty dog" ("Lyubka the Cossack"). Neither Froim Grach nor Lyubka seems to have stimulated Babel's imagination to quite the extent that Benya did. Consequently, "The Father" and "Lyubka the Cossack," though entertaining enough, do represent a certain falling away as compared with "The King" and "How It Was Done in Odessa." For this reason, possibly, no other such stories appeared in Babel's lifetime, though the action of the play *Sunset* takes place in the Moldavanka, and the stories "Sunset" and "Froim Grach" have been discovered and published posthumously.

Three other stories, all published in 1923, are humorously erotic in the manner of those written for Gorky's *Letopis'* seven years earlier. "Through the Fanlight" tells of a Peeping Tom who pays the madam of a brothel for the right to watch one of her girls, Marusya, at work. This he does by standing on a stepladder and peering through a convenient fanlight. One day, however, he slips and puts his fist through the glass. A tearful Marusya emerges from the bedroom with her client, to whom she shows affection beyond the call of duty. All is smoothed over, and the couple returns to the bedroom. The narrator, for twice the previous price, resumes his position at the fanlight and is both fascinated and surprised at the passion with which Marusya goes about her business.

"Story of a Woman" is more of a sexual tragicomedy. Ksenya has been widowed for three years, during which time she has behaved impeccably toward men. Eventually, however, her frustrations drive her for advice first to a doctor and then to the local wise woman, who arranges a rendezvous in the house where Ksenya is employed as a cook. Drink flows, but the prospective swain, far from becoming passionate, grows maudlin and offensive and eventually collapses. He has to be carried out, and Ksenya loses her job. Finally Ksenya and the wise woman are described weeping together, as another unfeeling day dawns.

"Chinky Chinaman" may also be classified as a sexual tragicomedy. In this story Babel depicted so tersely the relationship between a Leningrad prostitute, her elderly gentleman friend, and a Chinese client that any significance it may have is hard to descry. Perhaps its most impressive feature is the stylistic establishment of background. Babel succeeded brilliantly in creating the bleak atmosphere of the city shortly after the revolution—a bleakness that synchronizes with the behavior of the characters.

"The Sin of Jesus," published in 1924, is usually considered to be a revised version of "Story of a Woman," though the later work contains a completely new element with Christianity being mocked in a manner reminiscent of Pan Apolek's story in *Red Cavalry*. A hotel maid, Arina, whose lover, Seryoga, has to serve in the army for four years, seeks the advice of Jesus Christ. He offers to lend her an angel, Alfred, who will see to her needs in the absence of Seryoga. Unfortunately, during their first night together, the buxom and pregnant Arina embraces the puny Alfred so fiercely that he dies of suffocation, and the story ends with Arina bemoaning her lot and Christ asking her forgiveness in vain.

It cannot be claimed that any of these four stories possesses particular significance. In the main they confirm various aspects of Babel's art already apparent in his earlier work rather than reveal anything new about it. "Story of a Woman" and "The Sin of Jesus" represent further experiment with the *skaz* form. Each is narrated in conversational and colloquial style as though by a storyteller of no great education. As in "Mama, Rimma, and Alla" and "Il'ya Isaakovich and Margarita Prokof'yevna," sexual desire is the mainspring of grotesque situations, but by present-day standards none of the stories is more than mildly titillating, and Babel went into little or no sexual detail. His tone remains amusedly dry and detached, adding to the humor, but limiting the pathos that certainly exists in the case of Ksenya and in the triangular situation of "Chinky Chinaman." As in Gogol's work there is a mixture of laughter and tears, but the emphasis is on the former rather than the latter, and sentimentality is avoided.

Another two stories belonging to 1923 have affinity with *Red Cavalry*. Grishchuk, a cart driver, appears twice in the sequence. The story named after him, however, though first advertised as part of *Red Cavalry*, was not included in a single edition. Probably this was due to Babel's dissatisfaction, as it reads more like one of his early drafts than a complete and polished entity. Grishchuk's unusual past, conveyed rather flatly, fails to make maximum impact, and although the enigma of his personality is solved, this is not accomplished by those artistic means of which Babel had proved himself capable.

Babel gave to "There Were Nine of Them" the date August 1923. Still awaiting its first publication in Russia, the story bears such a close resemblance to "Squadron Commander Trunov" in *Red Cavalry*, that it may be regarded as an earlier version. Jewish, bespectacled, and attached to the Cossack cavalry fighting in Poland, the narrator seems identical with Lyutov. Conflict arises between him and the Cossacks over the treatment of prisoners. The narrator wishes to be humane; the Cossacks, impatient to strip them of their clothes, can only think of killing. Compared with "Squadron Commander Trunov," this story places more emphasis on the plight of the captured, and there are no extenuating circumstances to lessen the enormity of the Cossacks' behavior. The ending, not used in the later story, is striking. The narrator watches two Cossacks plunder hives, killing many bees in so doing. This wanton destruction parallels the shooting of prisoners, and the concluding lines express succinctly and movingly all his despair: "At the large number of memorials yet to be written I felt horrified." Far superior to "Grishchuk," this neglected story shows Babel near his best and deserves to be more widely known.

"Bagrat-Ogly and the Eyes of His Bull," which first appeared in 1923, has also been neglected, though with more reason. A slight, somewhat static piece, it possesses curiosity value as the only story in which Babel attempted to parody the style of Eastern legends. The account of the gelding of Bagrat-Ogly's bull by a jealous neighbor seems primarily an excuse for Babel to experiment in the manner of the so-called Russian Ornamentalists of the 1920s, in whose writings an elaborate and high-flown style tended to take precedence over subject matter. For all its unusual flavor, however, it is linked closely with the main body of Babel's work by the atmosphere of violence and fear developed in all but the concluding lyrical paragraph.

"Line and Color" is quite different, and its oddly effective blend of political and aesthetic observation also sets it apart from anything else Babel wrote. In part the story stands as a token of Babel's loyalty to the revolution, commenting on the shortcomings of Alexander Kerensky, prime minister in the Second Provisional Government and commander-in-chief of the Russian army during the insurrection of October 1917. Unhappily, though, from this angle, Kerensky is unfavorably compared at the very end with Trotsky, who was to suffer disgrace a few years later and whose name was to disappear in subsequent editions.

As regards aesthetics, the story records an argument on the relative merits of line and color. The argument is between Kerensky and the narrator at a meeting in Finland in December 1916. Though admitting to short-sightedness, Kerensky refuses to wear eyeglasses—much to the astonishment of the narrator, who tells him what beauties of the Finnish landscape he is missing. Kerensky remains unashamed of his inability to distinguish the narrator's "divine line, mistress of the world": "What need have I for line when I have color? The whole world is for me a gigantic theater in which I am the only member of the audience without opera glasses." There follows an abrupt switch to June 1917, when next the two men find themselves together. Kerensky is delivering a typically emotional speech but fails to appreciate the mood of the crowd (because of his myopia) in complete contrast to Trotsky, who replaces him on the rostrum. A shrewd and forceful political viewpoint is thus estab-

lished eloquently and concisely in an unusual story that
is often quoted in evaluations of Babel's art.

"You Were Taken In, Captain" provides a relatively
simpler example of Babel paying political homage. Written and published in 1924, the year of Lenin's death, it
tells of a British steamer berthed in Odessa on the day of
his funeral. Three Chinese, two Negroes, and a Malay are
refused permission ashore by the captain. The bosun,
however, "a pillar of red flesh," helps them to disobey
orders. The final paragraphs bring out a contrast between the colored crew members battling their way
through a blizzard to take part in the funeral procession
and the captain, unaware of the bosun's deceit, drinking
brandy in his comfortable cabin. Though slight and pos-
sessing less than usual of Babel's stylistic polish, the
story does stand out from the vast corpus of Soviet
literary Leninolatry by virtue of an unusual and oblique
approach to the subject.

Of the remaining stories published in 1924, "With
Our Leader Makhno," though given a civil war background, brings to mind the erotic stories already mentioned in this chapter rather than those of *Red Cavalry*.
A Jewish girl has been raped by six followers of the
Ukrainian anarchist, but neither she nor the narrator
occupies the center of attention. Instead the events of the
previous night are conveyed by Kikin, a messenger boy,
who is regarded as something of a simpleton. Though dis-
illusioned with Makhno and his men, he shows no pity for
the girl. In fact he had helped to hold her down and
declined to take his turn only because he feared catching
venereal disease from one of her ravishers.

The narrator remains a silent observer throughout.
In his curiosity to see what the girl looks like the morn-
ing after the rape, he recalls the Peeping Tom in
"Through the Fanlight." The tone adopted in each story

is one of total moral detachment. In the earlier, however, the effect produced is comic; in the later it is cruel
and callous. Babel liked to shock. In "With Our Leader
Makhno" he succeeded in doing so less as a result of the
subject matter itself than of the deliberately casual and
heartless way in which it is related.

"The End of St. Hypatius" first appeared in *Pravda*
in 1924, with the subtitle "From a Diary." The narrator
visits a famous monastery at Kostroma on the Volga.
Aesthetically he is capable of being impressed. A church
"of indescribable beauty" is pictured lying "against the
smoky northern sky like a peasant woman's kerchief of
many colors embroidered with Russian flowers." Nevertheless, the narrator's mockery of the religion symbolized
by this beauty remains unimpaired. The Virgin in a
painting is described as "a thin woman with knees drawn
apart and breasts dangling like two useless green hands."
The narrator feels oppressed by the "sepulchral saints" of
the icons, which "weighed down my carefree heart with
the coldness of their deathly passions, and I barely escaped from them. . . ."

As in *Red Cavalry* Babel mingled sensitivity and
banter in matters of religion. As in *Red Cavalry*, too, he
revealed an acute sense of history, juxtaposing with relish
Russia's holy past and her thrusting postrevolutionary
present. In 1613 Muscovites had come to the monastery
imploring Mikhail Romanov to succeed as czar; in 1924
women from the Textile Workers' Union arrive to occupy
quarters there. By the end of the story the monastery gate
displays a signboard on which are posted among other
things the emblem of the union and the inevitable ham-
mer and sickle. The end of St. Hypatius, this bizarre
contrast suggests, has come indeed.

In 1925 Babel, as author of *Red Cavalry*, met with
general acclaim in Moscow. The publication of "The Story

of My Dovecote" and of "First Love" won him still further laurels. In these, as in his earliest known work,
"Childhood: At Grandmother's," he derived inspiration
from his childhood, going back to 1905, when he and his
narrator were only ten years of age and living in
Nikolayev.

"The Story of My Dovecote" is dedicated to Gorky.
In this way Babel was not only acknowledging a debt of
gratitude but at the same time invoking the spirit of
Childhood, the first part of Gorky's celebrated semiauto-
biographical trilogy. There are some finely perceived in-
sights into the mind of Babel's child hero as, for example, when purchases are made in preparation for his
entry into secondary school: "No one in the world senses
new things more keenly than children. Children shudder
at the smell of newness, like a dog at the scent of a hare,
and experience a madness which later, as adults, we call
inspiration." Moreover, Babel conceived the promising
idea of describing a pogrom from the viewpoint of some-
one too young to appreciate its full significance. The
idea, however, is realized only in part, and the reader is
aware more of a mature narrator looking back at an
early traumatic experience than of a ten-year-old boy
who is caught up in frightening and bewildering events.

Though covering no more than a dozen pages, "The
Story of My Dovecote" is one of the longest of Babel's
stories. This untypical wordiness results from background
detail relating to social setting and family history. In
this way Babel conveyed the pressures exerted upon a
Jewish boy by an ambitious father, the corruption and
anti-Semitism of the educational authorities, and the
misfortunes of the narrator's relatives. Most prominent
among the latter is great-uncle Shoyl: "His plump hands
were moist, covered in fish scales, and reeked of cold and
wonderful worlds." The "wonderful worlds" were opened

up by Shoyl's stories. In later life the narrator discovered them to be mostly lies, but as a child he was constantly fascinated by their extravagance.

The pogrom that occupies the second half of the story is memorably rendered in the customary Babel manner—a taut style reinforced by choice of detail and juxtaposition calculated to produce the maximum grotesque and horrific effect. The rioting and looting take the narrator unawares just after he has bought some doves, his reward for passing the secondary school examination. One of the most famous scenes in all Babel's work occurs when the crippled street trader Makarenko demands to see what is in the boy's sack. He is eager to buy looted goods and, disappointed to find only doves, fells the young narrator with the same hand in which he has clutched a bird: "The dove's tender entrails crept down my forehead, and I closed my one unspotted eye so as not to see the world stretching out before me. This world was small and terrible." The poignancy of the situation is sharpened by two other factors. In the first place, Makarenko is loved and trusted by the local children; and secondly, doves are the traditional symbols of peace. Babel reiterated that the world seen by his narrator lying on the ground was "small and terrible," and this observation can be applied very aptly to the kind of world he himself created in the majority of his stories.

Another memorable scene depicts Shoyl, who has been killed by the mob. Somebody has stuck one fish into his mouth and another into his fly. This example of Babel's wit gains in savagery by reference to one of the fish being still alive and struggling.

The violent atmosphere developed in "The Story of My Dovecote" is cleverly maintained in its sequel "First Love." Undoubtedly the latter story benefits because the social and historical background has been so unforgetta-

bly established already. On this occasion Babel evoked
the spirit of the famous nineteenth-century writer, Ivan
Turgenev, borrowing the title of one of his most deli-
cately written tales in which Vladimir, a middle-aged
bachelor, looks back to the time in his adolescence when
he fell in love with an older girl, Zinaida.

The largely autobiographical sketch, "Childhood: At
Grandmother's," makes mention of Babel reading the
Turgenev story. One scene particularly fired his youthful
imagination. The high point occurred when Zinaida was
struck with a whip by Vladimir's father, who, it dramatically transpires, has become her lover. A different combination of love and violence runs through the twentieth-
century variation, "First Love," where the object of boyish
passion is a young wife, Galina Rubtsov, who lives next
door to the narrator's family. Prior to the pogrom the
ten-year-old watches curiously and jealously from his
window as Galina and her officer-husband indulge in
love play, and one is inevitably reminded in a different
context of the adult narrator in "Through the Fanlight"
and "With Our Leader Makhno." After the pogrom the
Rubtsovs give refuge to their Jewish neighbors, and
Galina comforts the young son: "My head lay on Galina's
hip, and this hip lived and breathed."

Whereas the narrator's family is plagued with misfortune, the Rubtsovs are patently happy together. The
officer crawling on his knees and kissing the bruises on
his wife's legs contrasts with the Jewish patriarch kneel-
ing in the dirt and imploring a Cossack captain to protect
his property. (Lionel Trilling, assuming this latter incident to be autobiographical, sees it as predetermining
Babel's relationship with the Cossacks.) Thus, joyful sen-
suality and racial hatred are deliberately juxtaposed.
Each element of juxtaposition brings the child grief in
about equal measure, contributing to a nervous illness

and necessitating that he leave Nikolayev for Odessa. As I have suggested in chapter two, Babel was here tracing the origins of a neurasthenia from which he himself never recovered. To a large extent, therefore, "The Story of My Dovecote" and "First Love" are moving personal documents as well as being among the most impressive specimens of Babel's art.

The popularity of Babel with the reading public brought in its wake a personal dilemma that was not to be satisfactorily resolved during his lifetime. As a literary celebrity he found himself exposed to excessive publicity. Everyone wanted to know him, not least women, and in 1925 he embarked on an affair with an actress. Toward the end of the year his wife, Zhenya, left the Soviet Union for good and settled in Paris. Babel's only sister had already set up house in Brussels in February 1925 and was eventually joined by her mother in July 1926. They, too, never returned to Russia.

In the latter part of 1926, therefore, the relatives to whom Babel felt closest were all living abroad, and his pleas to them to come back met with no response. His unhappy situation had been aggravated by chronic asthma and also by lack of time for writing. In a letter to Brussels of 7 September 1926 he stated that, after an interruption of eighteen months, he was at last at work again. Most of his time during this period of literary inactivity had been claimed by film work that proved financially attractive but left largely unsatisfied his restless creative drive. The years 1926 and 1927 saw the publication of no new work by Babel. Indeed, in this respect, the period 1926-29 is strikingly barren.

Not until July 1927 did Babel obtain permission to visit his relatives in the west. Once it was obtained, however, he took full advantage, delaying his return to the Soviet Union until October 1928. For the most part he seems to have spent his time attempting to salvage his marriage. An insuperable obstacle was his unwillingness to swell the ranks of Russian émigrés. In resisting the family pressure brought to bear upon him over this matter, he appears to have been guided mainly by artistic considerations, fearing that to cut himself from his roots would mean draining the source of his literary inspiration. He was, moreover, afflicted by homesickness. In October 1927, for example, he wrote from Marseilles to his friend I. Livshits: "Spiritual life is nobler in Russia. I am poisoned by Russia, I long for it, I think only of Russia." To the same correspondent he wrote from Paris in January 1928: "As regards individual freedom, living here is marvellous, but we Russians yearn for the wind of great thoughts and great passions."

The year 1928 marked the publication of two new works by Babel—the first time any had come out since 1925. *Sunset*, a play with a Moldavanka background, is discussed in the following chapter. "A Hard-working Woman," on the other hand, is a story that unites two thematic strands from Babel's earlier publications: life with the anarchist leader, Makhno, and prostitution. The efforts of a woman to feed her family by sleeping regularly with three of the partisans are conveyed partly through an overall narrator, who remains unobtrusively in the background, and partly through the mouths of the men themselves. The total effect produced is one of melancholy, dreary and unrelieved, with even the trumpets in honor of Makhno's first night with a girl sounding doleful.

In July 1929 Babel's wife gave birth to a girl, Natasha (Nathalie), thus providing him with further cause to regret separation from his relatives in the west. At the time Babel was staying in Rostov and in fact spent most of his year working in the Ukraine. But no new work at all was published under his name in 1929.

At this point three other stories must be mentioned. Two were written during the 1920s and so, almost certainly, was the third, but none appeared in Russian until after his death.

"Sunset," dated 1924–25, is a Moldavanka story, in which the action takes place earlier than in any other similar work. The style, customary for this genre, is one of exaggerated, tongue-in-the-cheek formality. Though Benya Krik is among the characters, the emphasis is less on him than on his father, Mendel, who runs a down-at-heel carter's business and is depicted as mean, cunning, filthy, and possessed of remarkable physical strength. He and his wife (an equally repulsive character) are detested by their two sons, Benya and Lyovka, and their only daughter, Dvoyra, who determine to smash the old man's authority. The Krik children's plan is to take him unawares and overpower him physically. The plan, however, almost misfires, and victory is won only by the timely intervention of Dvoyra wielding a colander. Husband and wife are then kept virtual prisoners in their own home as the sons try to introduce some order into Mendel's chaotic affairs. His humiliation is complete when he makes an unsuccessful attempt to escape, and the story ends with Benya, firmly in control, forcing him to exchange his habitual rags for a decent suit.

Compared with the other Moldavanka stories, "Sunset" possesses less humor and less sparkle to lighten the violence and downright unpleasantness of the events and the participants, though, as before, Babel zealously refrained from anything resembling a moral judgment. The original ending has unfortunately been lost. Even allowing for this, however, the story is on the whole inferior to others with a similar setting, which may account for its neglect until initial publication in 1964. It was on this work, nevertheless, that Babel based his first play, to which he gave the same title.

The other two stories that had to await posthumous publication in the original Russian are "An Inquiry" and "My First Literary Fee." The former is undated, but its setting, the Georgian capital Tiflis (now Tbilisi), suggests that it was written during or shortly after Babel's stay there from 1922 to 1923. "My First Literary Fee," dated 1922–28, is a longer and more polished version of this story.

"An Inquiry" is presented by the author as an explanation to a reader of how he started his literary career. The place where this happened was Tbilisi, "the town of roses and mutton fat." At the time the narrator, aged twenty, lusted after a local prostitute, Vera, who, in her quest for trade, is likened to a Virgin Mary sailing through the streets on the prow of a boat. After plucking up courage to proposition her, the young man feels ashamed of his virginity and invents an implausible story about having been forced by circumstances to live with older homosexuals, who gave him no opportunity to dally with the opposite sex. While relating this fiction, he becomes so carried away that he begins to believe his own fantasy and to feel quite sorry for himself. Vera is impressed to the extent of looking on the narrator not as a client but as a "sister" and returning him the money, which he comes to regard as his first literary fee.

This story clearly belongs with those other works in which Babel presented sexual relations between men and women in a whimsically humorous light. He emphasized Vera's indifference to her client once a bargain has been struck and likens her preparations for bed to those of a surgeon before an operation. This detachment contrasts comically with her later ardor, when she is this time likened to a carpenter building a house for a fellow craftsman and making the shavings fly thick and fast.

"My First Literary Fee" tells essentially the same

story with the same principal characters. This time, however, it does not take the form of an answer to a reader and contains much more background information, principally of a bizarre nature. Since this additional detail contributes greatly to the atmosphere and is conveyed with an often masterly touch, it seems reasonable to conclude that "My First Literary Fee" is a later expanded variant of "An Inquiry."

In the longer story the twenty-year-old youth's desire for sex arises to a large extent from his living in a room next to that of two newlyweds. They thresh about in a noisy frenzy of love "followed by a silence as penetrating as the whine of a cannon ball." Fresh information is supplied about the narrator's longing to write and about the many stories he carries in his head and which lie on his heart "like toads on a stone." The interval between the conclusion of his bargain with Vera and their actually going to her room is here lengthened, with the result that his passion for intercourse turns to loathing. Finally, there is a more detailed description of Vera's quarters, which by their squalor further depress his spirits. Despite these changes, however, the humor of the story remains much the same as in "An Inquiry," with the difference that it receives fuller and more confident expression.

In the second half of the 1920s Babel, though publishing little that was new, did complete several stories that were to come out later. Undoubtedly the most important of his works during this period is the play, *Sunset*, which represented his first contribution to the Russian theater and an entirely new departure in his career. This and his only other known play, *Maria*, are considered separately in the next chapter.

6

Babel

the Dramatist

$\mathbf{B}$abel's early connections with the theater can only be surmised. A childhood romance with the medium is suggested in the story "Di Grasso," published in 1937. The fourteen-year-old narrator, who trades in tickets, is held spellbound by the performances of the star of a Sicilian touring company, but his youthful reactions constitute a flimsy basis for any assertions about Babel himself. Exactly why Babel turned his attention briefly to drama is also a matter of conjecture. His liaison with an actress, his work on film dialogue, a simple desire to test his talents in a new setting—all these are speculative factors.

Critics generally have concentrated almost exclusively on Babel the storyteller (especially on the author of *Red Cavalry*) and given Babel the dramatist little more than a polite nod. It is true that he is known to have written only two plays. It is true also that his mastery in the short story is not matched in his writings for the stage. Further, as I have mentioned already, there is an almost complete absence of data concerning his theatrical credentials. Yet none of these considerations excuses the reluctance both to examine at due length Babel's stature in the Soviet theater and to consider his plays in relation to the remainder of his work.

Sunset, Babel's first play, appeared in 1928. Almost immediately it received an enthusiastic welcome from a contributor, G. A. Gukovsky, to the first book of criticism entirely concerned with Babel's art: "At this very moment, when our new and still young drama is wandering in the dark and quite often straying from the right path, a drama by a writer such as Babel cannot fail to be an event. . . ." Later in the same year Stanislavsky's Moscow Art Theater gave *Sunset* its Russian premiere, although it had originally been performed first in Baku and then in Odessa in October 1927. The state of the Soviet theater in 1928 was, as Gukovsky suggests, not particularly healthy. Because of the more immediate impact drama can produce upon its audience, Soviet writers were permitted less latitude when creating plays than when creating novels, poems, or short stories. Toward the end of the 1920s, moreover, the Soviet writer found his freedom of expression becoming alarmingly circumscribed. After 1917 up until approximately the mid-1920s he had enjoyed comparatively wide scope, but, as Stalin's position at the apex of power grew more secure, so his grip on the organs of opinion tightened, and the situation of the writer began rapidly to deteriorate.

Nineteen twenty-eight marked the beginning of the First Soviet Five-Year Plan. Writers were enjoined to record the nation's future hopes and present achievements. Particular pressure came to be exerted upon so-called fellow-traveling writers (Babel among them), who gave at best only tepid support to the Communist party and its ambitious program. The play, *Sunset*, did not, however, treat of current events. Instead it harks back to the prerevolutionary Odessa of 1913 and to the narrow world of the Moldavanka. It is instructive to observe how the short-story writer adapted his talents and compositional habits to meet the exigencies of a different medium. Of course observation is enhanced by the recent discovery of the story from which the play developed. An essential feature of Babel's style is his brevity, whether applied to sentence structure or to plot, and though "Sunset" almost equals "The Story of My Dovecote" in length, it had to be expanded before a full-length play on the same subject could result. An unusual insight offered, therefore, by a comparison between story and play is of Babel working against his natural inclinations and adding to, rather than subtracting from, a particular work.

Brevity is attained in other ways, however. The play

consists of eight scenes, some extremely short and none especially long. The dialogue, moreover, reflects Babel's ingrained laconism, though with one important difference. In the story he uses dialogue more sparingly, providing most of the necessary background information through third-person narrative. A play, on the other hand, must rely almost entirely on dialogue to convey details of plot. For this reason Babel's stage characters speak at greater length, and the pithy and purposely formal-sounding witticisms of the story have to be interspersed with what, from the purely literary point of view, is rather more mundane material. As if to compensate for this dilution, Babel included detailed remarks about scenery, stage directions, and cast in the style of his short stories. It is as though he were anxious to sacrifice as little as possible of his proven technique on the altar of the theater and had determined to cater for his past readership as well as for the future playgoer.

While the plot of the drama remains fundamentally the same as in the short story, it is enriched by much that is new. Nowhere can this better be illustrated than by reference to Mendel Krik, whose characterization is deepened and whose attempts to defy his advanced years acquire additional pathos. More than before Babel isolated him within his own family. In the earlier version he could always count for support on his wife, but in the play she fulfills a smaller and more sympathetic role, resenting her husband's tyranny just as much as do her children.

Before Mendel appears on stage, the violence of the opposition to his patriarchal authority has already been demonstrated. Dvoyra, his "overripe" daughter, becomes hysterical over the disappearance of a favorite dress. She is expecting a prospective suitor, Boyarsky, but not for the first time Mendel has tried to wreck her chances of marriage, as he is too mean to supply a dowry. Both her brothers sympathize. Lyovka, the younger, voices open contempt for Mendel, while the gaudily clad Benya says little but hovers menacingly in the background.

The patriarch is introduced in person with powerful dramatic effect. He enters carrying a whip, casts it aside and sits down in silence for his wife to remove his boots. Totally ignoring Boyarsky, he questions an employee about Lyovka's impudence in giving orders without his father's permission. As a sign of displeasure he then sweeps everything off the kitchen table and declares his sole authority over the household and the business before storming out. The inevitability of a clash between Mendel and his children is further emphasized in the following scene (which did not appear in the original story), when Benya commits the unheard of act of entering his parents' bedroom at night to complain of the noise.

Another completely new scene set in a tavern successfully puts Mendel's position in perspective and gives his characterization an extra dimension. As at home he acts the petty despot, behaving violently when his commands are not obeyed and disporting himself destructively without any thought for others. In a drunken state, however, he also reveals self-deception and inability to face facts, for despite his sixty-two years he still believes himself invincible. His dream is to start a new life in Bessarabia with a twenty-year-old mistress, Marusya. Here we see a change from the plot of the short story in which Benya made pregnant a girl of the same name, but Mendel was not shown as anything but a faithful spouse. Another fresh factor is Mendel's decision to sell his carter's business without consulting his sons, and this finally precipitates against him the smoldering family revolt.

Again new light is shed on Mendel's character in the fourth scene, which cleverly conveys his infatuation with Marusya. Whereas previously he has been depicted as brutal and dictatorial, here he shows himself gentle, submissive, and even pitiable. As the girl and old man prepare for bed, she chatters away nonstop, while the solitary word he utters during the entire proceedings is the affectionate diminutive of her name.

Only in the fifth scene, set in a synagogue, does Mendel not make an appearance. It is at this juncture that Benya learns of his father's intention to sell up and move away. In the scene that follows, the long-threatened confrontation between Mendel and his sons takes place at last. As in the story, he proves physically more than a match for them, but Dvoyra's intervention is not called upon this time, Benya resolving the struggle with a blow from his revolver. Stage directions throughout indicate with no great subtlety what is to ensue as well as underlining the significance of what has happened already. The scene begins at sunset. When the fighting breaks out, "the sky is bathed in blood. . . ." Immediately after Mendel's defeat, the sun sinks still lower. The final direction rounds off the scene as follows: "Silence. Evening. A blue darkness, but above the darkness the sky is still purple, set in a glow, and pitted with cavities of fire."

In the last two scenes Benya becomes the focus of attention in his new capacity as head of the family. Mendel, on the other hand, has been transformed into a dispirited wreck of a man whose "face is blue and swollen like the face of a corpse." As in the short story, this transition is too total and too sudden to surprise in an entirely convincing way. As in the story, too, Lyovka protests at Benya's ill treatment of Mendel, who laments his lost power and begs for freedom in one of the play's most emotionally charged speeches:

Why won't you unlock the gate . . . ? Why won't you let me out of the yard in which I have passed my life? (The old man's voice strengthens and a light blazes at the base of his eyes.) It has seen me, this yard, a father to my children, a husband to my wife, and a master over my horses. It has seen my strength, my twenty stallions, my twelve ironbound drays. It has seen my legs, as large as pillars, and my arms, my devilishly strong arms. . . . And now open up for me, dear sons, let today be as I want it. Let me out of this yard that has seen too much. . . .

His appeal, however, remains unheeded, and the scene ends with another elderly Jew (Ar'ye-Leyb of "How It Was Done in Odessa") likening Mendel's insatiable appetites to those of the aging King David.

In the final scene Benya celebrates his triumph by throwing a party. Only toward the end of it does Mendel enter and even then is allowed but a single remark. Significantly Benya interrupts him to announce his father's gift of a large sum to charity—a gesture quite out of keeping with Mendel's nature but one calculated to win Benya admiration and popularity. From now on it is the oldest son who rules the family, having reduced its former despotic head to the status of an impotent subject. In conclusion the most distinguished guest, Ben Zkhar'ya, the local rabbi (who does not figure in the original story), pronounces the last word in the play and draws a somewhat commonplace moral with regard to Mendel's fate:

All his life he wanted to bake in the heat of the sun, all his life he wanted to stand in the place where midday had found him. But God has policemen in every street and Mendel Krik had sons in his home. Policemen come and impose order. Day is day, and evening is evening. Everything is as it should be, Jews. Let us drink a glass of vodka!

Most of the differences between the play and the story arise from the fuller characterization of Mendel.

This involves in turn a wider variety of scenes and a larger cast of characters with the result that the Jewish ambience is conjured up in greater density. Basically, however, the play has much in common with the Moldavanka stories and Babel's other earlier work as regards both tone and technique. Though making unavoidable concessions to the theater medium, he succeeded in other ways already mentioned in maintaining his characteristic economy of expression. Moreover, the aura of violence pervading his Moldavanka and *Red Cavalry* stories is established from the very beginning of the play, and the ultimate explosion in the sixth scene is if anything excessively prepared for and delayed. As before, Babel depicted an exotic jungle of a community in which only the strong and ruthless flourish. Idiosyncratic juxtapositions are used as ever to jolt the reader. In the synagogue scene talk of moneymaking and a proposed robbery mingle with the prayers of the congregation; and Ar'ye-Leyb's instruction of a child in the scriptures precedes the decisive battle between the Kriks. Of the typically grotesque details in the play the most curious occurs when the cantor in the synagogue, finding his complaints about rats going unheeded, pulls out a revolver and shoots one during the service! Another memorably bizarre phenomenon is the choir of blind Jews that sings for Mendel in the tavern.

Apart from the bedroom scene between Marusya and Mendel there is little erotic content of the kind to be found in several earlier (and later) works. A more striking difference is the moral expounded by the rabbi at the end, which sounds strange coming as it does from an author mostly at pains to refrain from judgments of any sort. A final distinction between the play and the Moldavanka tales specifically is that the larger-than-life characters of the tales (especially Benya) assume more human proportions when appearing in the flesh and speaking for themselves. *Sunset* the play tends therefore to be a little less extravagant and a little more down-to-earth than "Sunset" the short story.

Compared with most other new plays staged in the late 1920s *Sunset* seemed something of an anachronism. Not only was it essentially remote from the revolution in subject and spirit, but also it did not lend itself easily to a socio-political interpretation advantageous to the Soviet régime. P. Markov, a critic respected by Babel, could view the play as an attack upon the Moldavanka way of life only by disregarding that there is no more evidence of condemnation here than in the earlier stories and that the triumphant Benya is hardly a positive hero dedicated to building socialism.

Sunset remains far superior to most other dramas of the time in the quality of its writing, though perhaps more impressive as literature to be read than a play to be performed. Babel expressed disappointment that the first production had failed to convey those subtleties he believed present beneath its surface, and Markov, a member of the Moscow Art Theater, perceived a conflict of attitude between author and producer, declaring himself on Babel's side. Ominously, however, he found the play's philosophy alien to the epoch and after sixteen performances it disappeared from the repertory.

Babel's second play, *Maria*, forsakes prerevolutionary Odessa for postrevolutionary Leningrad. The action is said to take place "during the early years of the revolution," but a reference to the likelihood of war with Poland indicates 1920. The place and period chosen offered not only rich dramatic possibilities but also ample scope for a writer with Babel's stylistic tendencies.

The year 1920 was one of political uncertainty, social transition and economic hardship. Although the Bolsheviks controlled much of the country, particularly the large cities, the civil war was by no means won and a new way of life was still emerging from the chrysalis. Babel recreated the atmosphere of the period by concentrating mainly on representatives of the old order, over whose future in a socialist society hung a disturbing question mark. Those who had decided to remain in Russia are shown adapting to radically changed circumstances in a variety of ways. A former prince, Golitsyn, literally scrapes a living by playing the cello in taverns and finds dockers most appreciative of his sad melodies. An un-named professor is mentioned as having entered the sausage trade since the revolution. Dymshits, a Jew, smuggles in black-market goods with the aid of maimed war veterans. His girlfriend, Lyudmila Mukovnin, thinks only of having a good time and exploits her beauty to obtain it. In contrast, her elder sister, Maria, works self-lessly in the political section of the Red Army and is attached to a division commanded by a former black-smith. The fates of these and other characters are played out against a background of privation and fear, with the necessities of life in short supply and people afraid to walk in the streets at night lest they be stripped of the clothes they stand in.

The juxtaposition of old and new had been a feature of *Red Cavalry*. In *Maria* it consists in examining how former privileged persons survive at a time when their privileges have ceased and they themselves are in danger of being trampled underfoot by the class upon whose oppression their high standard of living had once de-pended. From their point of view the situation had the quality of a nightmare. Babel increased the general lurid-ness by a selection of physiological details that connote decay and disintegration: the grotesquely mutilated bodies of Dymshits's accomplices; the rape of Lyudmila by Viskovsky, a former army officer; and Lyudmila's consequent venereal disease. Unfortunately, in attempting to shock, Babel veered into melodrama that is not only more acceptable in the exotic world of the Moldavanka but was also more skillfully handled for the theater in his earlier play, *Sunset*. For example, the shooting of Viskovsky is poorly motivated, and the writhing of General Mukovnin during a heart attack contributes little or nothing by taking place on stage. Both instances were intended as powerful dramatic situations prior to the fall of the curtain but risk arousing nervous laughter rather than horror.

Maria recalls *Sunset* in its length and its eight scenes. On the whole, however, it is the inferior play, as regards not only tone but also construction. The heroine, Maria, never in fact appears, and, though her expected arrival in the seventh scene does engender considerable tension, it leads also to a theatrically stagnant fifth scene devoted almost entirely to the reading aloud of a letter she has sent from the Ukrainian front. Babel here firmly established her idealism, contrasting it with the selfishness and emptiness of Lyudmila and other characters who had been nurtured by the czarist régime, but he did so in a somewhat crude literary manner and utilized none of the potentialities offered by the stage medium.

Some characters who do appear in person possess little more substance than the absent heroine. Golitsyn, the former nobleman who takes refuge in religion, remains an interesting embryonic character insufficiently developed; the depraved Viskovsky never really comes to life; and Dymshits contributes nothing new to Babel's gallery of Jewish rogues. Babel's love of brevity served him less well here than in *Sunset*, where the Moldavanka milieu had already become familiar through earlier stories, and the extravagant conduct of the characters was more or less acceptable in context. In setting his play in Leningrad at such a complex period of history, however, Babel

needed to concentrate on fewer characters or alternatively
to expand the play's length if he were to do justice to his
theme.

The final scene of *Maria*, in which preparations are in
train for a working family to move into the Mukovnins'
former apartment, does not entirely succeed. Obviously
such an ending aims to emphasize the rapid and radical
nature of social change at the time in question, but to
introduce so many new characters at such a late stage
requires more theatrical expertise than Babel possessed,
and the play concludes somewhat lamely in consequence.
In sum, though full of interest for Babel's view of 1920,
Maria does represent a technical regression by comparison
with *Sunset*.

In a letter to his mother and sister in May 1933
Babel described *Maria* as a herculean task that would
probably bring him trouble because it did not accord with
the party line. His fears proved all too justified. Though
allowed to appear in print in March 1935, it incurred
official displeasure and was eventually excluded from the
repertory. Like *Sunset* in 1928, *Maria* may be regarded as
alien to the philosophy of the epoch. In this instance
Babel failed to meet the requirements of Soviet socialist
realism, which commended works revealing the positive
side of Russian life and deplored those featuring promi-
nently scenes of sex and violence. The total absence of
his positive heroine from the action suggests that any attempt to compromise with the new literary doctrine was at
most half-hearted. On the other hand, the critic I.
Lezhnev wrote, in an unenthusiastic review accompanying
the original published text of the play, that it represented
the first part of a trilogy and that Maria would eventually
appear in person. As far as is known, however, the other
two parts never materialized and Babel's career as a
dramatist ended briefly and unfortunately.

In the history of the Soviet theater Babel stands out as an unusual and isolated figure. Unsurprisingly, in view of his relative lack of experience, he was not entirely at ease with the medium. Nevertheless, in only two plays he revealed unmistakable stage talent, and it is a matter for regret that he did not continue to enliven the Stalinist theater and relieve the general mediocrity of the drama it produced.

7

The Last Years
(1930-1941?)

Of all Babel's works published during the 1930s *Maria* was the most ambitious. Apart from a few articles, the remaining publications consisted of miscellaneous short stories that do not make up a cohesive body of work but still merit examination for the way Babel made further use of old settings and tried his hand at new.

In any estimate of Babel's achievement during this period the critic must admit the presence of an imponderable factor—namely, that most of Babel's work dating from 1934 appears to have been destroyed. Erenburg, for example, writes of a novel on which Babel had been engaged during his last years. Moreover, Antonina Pirozhkov, who from 1935 on lived with Babel as his wife, mentions two novels he had been near to finishing (one of them featured a hero who had worked as both collective farmer and miner and whose characterization had much in common with Benya Krik's). The disappearance of these manuscripts not only denies us insight into how Babel coped with a new genre (although the fragment, "The Jewess," may well be part of a novel) but also means that any consideration of his work during the 1930s must inevitably remain incomplete.

With the possible exception of the period 1946–53, when Stalin was paranoiac to the point of insanity, the 1930s brought more tribulation to Soviet writers than any other postrevolutionary period. During this decade the artist found himself subject to unbending political discipline, and the previous diversity in Russian literature gave way to depressingly predictable uniformity. Fear became terror as a consequence of arbitrary purges from which no citizen could feel safe—not even the purgers themselves— and to which artists were especially vulnerable. Apart from his vocation, Babel suffered two additional handicaps. Firstly, he had relatives living in western Europe, which made him automatically suspect. Secondly, he was a Jew under a dictator whose anti-Semitic prejudices grew more pronounced with time.

A portent of trouble ahead was the accusation in 1930 that during his sojourn abroad Babel had given an interview to a Polish poet on the French Riviera and spoken of the impossibility of working freely in the Soviet Union. Babel denied the charge and the Federation of Soviet Writers' Organizations officially cleared him, but the incident was a straw in a wind of ill omen.

Nineteen-thirty proved a blank year for new publications by Babel. In 1931, however, four original stories appeared—twice as many as during the previous five years!

"Gapa Guzhva" was presented by Babel as the first chapter of *Velikaya Krinitsa*, which may have been one of the novels referred to by Antonina Pirozhkov. It seems, however, a quite complete entity in the form of a short story. The background to the work is the collectivization of agriculture. In February 1930 Babel wrote to his mother and sister that he was leaving Kiev for the countryside to witness at first hand the revolutionary transformation of village life. "Gapa Guzhva," however, is far from being a paean to Soviet economic progress, as was so much other literature produced during the period of the First Soviet Five-Year Plan. The efforts of party officials are very much subordinate to Babel's observation of peasant customs and to his characterization of Gapa herself. With relish he described the ceremonies following no less than six weddings on the same day in a village where only twenty years before the matchmaker had been deprived of his right to "try" the bride. Other ancient traditions have survived, however. Sheets, stained with the maidenhead blood, must be raised over the cottages where the newlyweds spent their first night together. There then ensues a competition to see who can fetch them down and claim the reward of food and drink. Only two of the six couples are able to display sheets properly embellished, and one of the successful competitors is Gapa Guzhva, a lusty extrovert widow of the same pedigree as Lyubka the Cossack with the reputation of having seduced most of the lads in the village.

Even at the meeting of the village council Babel allows Gapa to overshadow Osmolovsky and Ivashko, who have been sent by the Communist party to introduce collectivization and are encountering stubborn opposition. Her concern with the advent of a new system is entirely of a sexual nature, as she jokes about rumors that collectivization will require everyone to sleep under the same blanket. Finally she pays a nocturnal visit to Osmolovsky to inquire about the kind of life a sexual freebooter like herself can expect in the village of the future.

Despite the change of milieu and the consequent use of peasant speech, "Gapa Guzhva" differs little in essence from Babel's earlier stories. Political and economic factors play no great part, and, judged by its opening chapter, the projected novel would have given collectivization very oblique treatment. Compared with other works on the same subject written at about the same time (for example, the first volume of Sholokhov's *Virgin Soil Upturned*), "Gapa Guzhva" lacks serious socio-political intent. In it Babel stands revealed as a writer who, for all the pressure exerted on him, was a leopard unwilling or unable to change his literary spots.

According to Babel's own dating, "Gapa Guzhva" was written in the spring of 1930. So, too, was "Kolyvushka," which also treats of collectivization but did not appear during his lifetime. Babel subtitled it "from a novel *Velikaya Staritsa*," but the reappearance of a few of the inhabitants of Velikaya Krinitsa suggests it may be a fragment from the same work as "Gapa Guzhva." The tone of "Kolyvushka" is more sober and more violent, but as in "Gapa Guzhva," the character most to the fore is no paragon of socialist rectitude. After the newly formed *kolkhoz* (collective farm) has appropriated his property, Kolyvushka finds himself, for reasons unspecified, debarred from membership. His immediate reaction to this decision is a destructive one—killing a mare with foal and smashing a seeding machine. Such is his agitation that he turns gray overnight, and, after being threatened by the head of the village council, he leaves Velikaya Staritsa, never to return.

An atmosphere of brooding violence is conveyed throughout this sparely written story. The party men are not drawn particularly sympathetically and do not emerge as heroes. Babel focused instead upon a casualty of collectivization and only to that limited extent reflects the social significance of what was happening to Soviet agriculture.

Two of the stories published in 1931 tell of an Odessan childhood. The narrator is the same as in "The Story of My Dovecote" and "First Love." "In the Basement" features him at the age of twelve living in poor surroundings with his crazy grandfather, quarrelsome uncle, and understanding aunt. The eccentricity of his forebears is made to seem grotesquely colorful:

Here it must be said that the family from which I came was not as other Jewish families. Some members had been drunkards; some had seduced generals' daughters and abandoned them before reaching the frontier; our grandfather had forged signatures and written blackmailing letters for deserted wives.

Solace comes to the lonely boy narrator through the world of books and through the world of his own imagination. He feels ashamed of his relatives, inventing stories about them for the benefit of his closest friend, Mark

Borgman, the son of a Jewish banker. When Mark visits the narrator in his basement home, uncle and grandfather have been got rid of beforehand but ruin everything by returning too soon. The frantic host tries to drown the noise of quarreling by declaiming at the top of his voice Antony's speech over Caesar's corpse. Literature again becomes a substitute for life, but on this occasion to no avail, and Mark leaves in embarrassed haste.

As in "The Story of My Dovecote" and "First Love," Babel recaptured agonizingly the pain of child-hood. This time, however, it stemmed from social inferi-ority—from the disparity in wealth and status between the families of the narrator and his friend, and from the shame the narrator feels for his unfortunate relatives. At the end of the story he tries to drown himself in a water barrel, and, failing in this, expresses his misery in the only other way available to him: "Then for the first time that day I began to cry, and the world of tears was so huge and wonderful that everything but tears disappeared from my eyes."

The theme of literature in this story distinguishes it from its predecessors and casts possible light upon the sources of Babel's own creative urge. The narrator's love of reading and devising far-fetched tales is shown as a means of escaping from an unpleasant reality and bears affinity to his great-uncle Shoyl's unlikely but fascinating stories in "The Story of My Dovecote" as well as to "The Headless Man," the work his grandfather is writing. Here, thinly disguised, seems to be a personal record of the making of a writer and of the circumstances that formed his particular vision.

The story "Awakening" tells of the same narrator a year or so afterwards and especially of the conflict between his father's musical ambitions for him and his own literary propensities. Reluctantly he joins the ranks of the undersized would-be prodigies of the violin: "Among that sect I was out of my element. Just as much a dwarf as the rest of them, I discerned in the voice of my ancestors inspiration of a different kind."

The narrator reads novels instead of sheet music and eventually ceases to attend classes altogether, preferring the attractions of the harbor. Here he meets the newspaper proofreader, Nikitich, a sympathetic old man, who not only teaches the boy to swim but also reads his work and gives shrewd advice:

"What bird is that singing?"
I could give no reply. The names of trees and birds, the species to which they belonged, where birds fly to, from what direction the sun rises, when the dew is at its heaviest —all this was a mystery to me.
"And yet you dare to write? . . . Anyone who doesn't live in nature, as a stone or an animal do, won't write two worthwhile lines all his life. . . . Your landscapes are like descriptions of stage scenery. God alive, what have your parents been thinking of these fourteen years? . . ."
What had they been thinking of? . . . Of protested bills of exchange, of the private residences of Misha El'man. . . . I didn't say that to Nikitich but held my tongue.

As in the other three stories of childhood, "Awakening" ends with its narrator deep in misery. His father's wrath on discovering his absence from music lessons causes him to seek sanctuary in the toilet, and, when everything has calmed down, he is finally led away to the safety of his grandmother's. The story, however, is concerned less with the boy's domestic unhappiness than with the awakening of his senses to the natural world, of which, prior to Nikitich's influence, he had been only vaguely aware. The necessity for exact observation has been impressed upon a budding writer, and this story records memorably another stage in his development.

"Karl-Yankel" is also set in Odessa, though after the revolution. Basic to this story is one of Babel's favorite themes—the struggle between the old and the new—which receives here primarily humorous treatment. At the center of the struggle is a Jewish baby. His father, a candidate party member, wants to call him Karl in honor of Marx. On the other hand his grandmother determines to call him Yankel and takes advantage of her son-in-law's absence to have the child circumcised.

A notable addition to Babel's comic repertoire is the circumciser, Naftula Gerchik, whose eccentric working methods are gleefully related. During the court case brought by the child's father he reminds public prosecutor Orlov (formerly Zusman) of his own circumcision some thirty years before: "And now we see that you've become a big man under Soviet rule and that Naftula didn't take away with that piece of nonsense anything which might have helped you later on. . . ."

Babel wasted no opportunity of puncturing the solemnity of the legal proceedings, as in the cross examination of the baby's mother:

"Tell us, witness . . . were you aware of your husband's decision to call your son Karl?"
"I was."
"What did your mother call him?"
"Yankel."
"And you, witness, what did you call your son?"
"I called him 'poppet.' "
"Why 'poppet' exactly? . . ."
"I call all children 'poppet.' "

The need for the baby to be fed (its cry makes the Red Army guards reach for their rifles!) enforces a recess, and at the end of the story the case has still not been resolved. In conclusion the unobtrusive narrator reflects wryly on his own childhood and how no one had fought over him as over this child.

Babel's characteristic refusal to adopt a moral posture offended the sensibilities of Jewish and Communist faithful alike. By his frivolous treatment of a delicate issue he found he had stirred up something of a hornet's next. Reacting with wounded surprise, he attempted to play down both the merit and importance of a work that displayed dangerous disregard for the political mood of the time.

In 1932 four more new stories by Babel were published. One of these, "The End of the Poorhouse," takes place, like "Karl-Yankel," in postrevolutionary Odessa. The initial situation is startlingly paradoxical, with the inmates of a poorhouse flourishing at a time of acute material hardship. Their salvation lies in a combination of two factors: the shortage of timber and the ancient Jewish custom according to which a corpse must lie in a coffin until burial but is lowered into the grave in a shroud only. By hiring out a coffin of their own and monopolizing the duties performed in the cemetery next door, the paupers prosper. Their main source of income dries up, however, when the precious coffin is buried together with a Red officer, and the remainder of the story shows them struggling to regain their former standard of living.

Two characters from previous Odessan stories reappear in "The End of the Poorhouse"—Ar'ye-Leyb, who narrates most of "How It Was Done in Odessa" and has a role in the play *Sunset*; and Simon-Wol'f, the fractious uncle of the narrator of "In the Basement." These two are prominent in pressing the poorhouse superintendent to improve the lot of themselves and their fellows. Though the paupers seem at one time to have carried the day, they are eventually evicted, and the final scene is of aged tatterdemalions trudging sadly away from their relative paradise under the guard of Red soldiers.

The idea of people with one foot in the grave living well while thousands younger and healthier starved is bizarre even by Babel's standards. In "The End of the Poorhouse" there is concentration upon remnants of an old way of life that seem deliberately chosen for their incongruity. It is as though Babel had been viewing a confused and in many ways terrible moment in history through the wrong end of binoculars. The result is a complete absence of perspective but a gain in that nightmarish brightness that dazzles in so many of Babel's stories.

Two of the stories published in 1932 refer to the early years of revolution and belong to the province of semi-autobiography. "The Journey" can be divided into two main parts. The first describes the Jewish narrator's journey from Kiev to Leningrad at the beginning of 1918. When his train is stopped for the examination of documents an outbreak occurs of anti-Semitic hysteria. Without warning, a harmless Jewish teacher is shot and his genitals cut off and stuffed into the mouth of his newly-wedded wife—surely the most horrifying incident to be found in all Babel's work and one usually omitted in modern editions. Other Jews are thrown onto the track, and the narrator himself is turned off the train after being stripped of boots and overcoat. Eventually he staggers to a hospital, but not before his feet are so frozen that at one time amputation appears necessary.

The second part of "The Journey" is a revised version of "An Evening at the Empress's" (1922). Having reached Leningrad, the narrator seeks out a former army comrade, Kalugin, now working for the Cheka in the Anichkov Palace. Much amusement is derived from his sacrilegious behavior amid unaccustomed opulence—he wears a dressing gown of the former emperor, Alexander

III (noting with surprise its patched and soiled state), smokes the rare imperial cigars, and examines the boyish belongings of Nicholas II. In his imagination is resurrected a past world seeming in direct contrast to that which rages beyond the palace walls, but in reality linked to it closely by chains of history.

"The Journey" ends with the narrator working for the Cheka as a translator. "The S. S. *Cow-Wheat*" finds him in the summer of 1918 requisitioning grain at Baronsk, capital of the Volga Germans. In this longest of Babel's known short stories he took his time setting the scene and recording the reactions of the requisitioners to the "Russian California". These men, newly arrived from starving Leningrad, stuff themselves with so much bread at first as to suffer "blissful indigestion" for the next fortnight. A grim reminder of the strain imposed on Russian manpower ever since 1914 is the presence among the requisitioners of many disabled. Showing, as ever, a penchant for the grotesque, Babel described how in leisure hours they often combined to perform as one—as, for example, when two one-legged men swim together!

The main story, however, concerns not the grain collectors but the steamer, *Cow-Wheat*, which carries arms and ammunitions for the Reds. The narrator and a friend happen to be on board when the drunken captain, Korostelyov, lifts anchor to fetch home-brewed vodka from the nearest village known to make it. Almost all members of the crew have been drinking heavily and supplies are exhausted. A nightmare trip ends when the steamer crashes into the landing stage on its return to Baronsk, where Red soldiers are waiting. Without more ado their commander almost casually shoots Korostelyov for the unforgivable crime at this time of wasting fuel, and the rest of the sailors are arrested.

"The S. S. *Cow-Wheat*" suggests quite successfully

the tense situation obtaining during the early days of the Russian civil war. As ever Babel's approach remained tangential, as he stood on the fringe of great events, weaving together documentary and anecdote. Nowadays, modern Soviet compilers of his selected works tend to exclude this story. Consequently, it is far less well known than its qualities merit.

The fourth of Babel's stories published in 1932 was "Guy de Maupassant." Much of the background is autobiographical: the Jewish narrator's penniless state in the Leningrad of 1916, and his feeling for the work of Maupassant. He helps an attractive Jewess, Raisa, to translate Maupassant for an edition to be brought out by her wealthy husband. From this situation two themes develop that were dear to Babel's heart: one literary, the other amorous.

The literary theme is of interest for Babel's pronouncements on style. For example, after touching up Raisa's lifeless versions, the narrator comments: "This work is not as bad as it seems. A phrase is born into the world good and bad at the same time. The secret lies in a twist barely perceptible. The lever must lie in the hand and grow warm there. It must be turned once, but not twice." When asked by Raisa to explain why his translations are so much better than hers, he begins to speak "of style, of the army of words, of the army in which all kinds of weapons are brought into action," and there then follows the already quoted remark about the devastating power of a carefully timed full stop.

The amorous theme arises mainly from the admiration for Raisa of the young narrator, who is constantly subject to sexual fantasies. When, in an intoxicated condition, both read from Maupassant's *L'aveu*, art spills over into life, and the narrator, quoting from the story, tries to make love to her. Whether he succeeds in doing so is not made clear but seems likely, judging by his high spirits on

returning home. There he picks up a biography of Maupassant and finishes it at a sitting. The account of Maupassant's hereditary syphilis and resultant madness makes
a particular impression upon him, and the final paragraph
of Babel's story follows: "I read the book to the end and
got up from the bed. A fog had come up to the window
and hidden the universe. My heart contracted. A presenti-
ment of the truth had touched me." The whole tone of
the story changes in these lines as the young man begins
to realize that immense suffering often forms the basis of
great art. The Babel of 1932 was reasonably qualified to
speak on the subject. Here, however, in this subtly modu-
lated story with an unexpected conclusion he discovered
the truth afresh through the mind and eyes of inexperi-
ence.

In September 1932 Babel made his second trip
abroad. Most of the time was spent with his wife and
daughter in Paris, and as before he remained absent from
the Soviet Union for about a year. In April 1933 he
traveled via Naples to Gorky's home in Sorrento, from
where, at the beginning of May, he announced the com-
pletion of his play *Maria*. Later that month Babel took
the opportunity to visit Naples (for the second time),
Rome, and Florence, but an urgent summons to Paris in
connection with a film script hastened his return. In
August he finally left for the Soviet Union, where
rumors, which he described as "absurd but sinister," had
been circulating about him.

It was during 1933 that expurgation of Babel's works
began. This was directed chiefly against erotic elements
and against passages (such as that in "The Journey")
considered *outré*. Not until the publication of the stories
"Oil" and "Dante Street" in 1934 did anything new of
his appear.

"Oil" is unusual in the Babel canon for being narrated in the first person by a woman and given an indus-

trial setting toward the end of the First Soviet Five-Year
Plan. In common with several stories from *Red Cavalry*,
it takes the form of a letter and bristles with up-to-date
Soviet jargon. Claudia, the writer of the letter, emerges as
a tough, confident specimen of "the new Soviet woman,"
who holds a responsible post in the oil industry. Inter-
twined with her picture of a country proceeding at full
technological throttle is the fate of a pregnant unmarried
woman of aristocratic origin. Her doubts about having the
baby are ridiculed by Claudia in breathless style:

Always the same reply: "I can't let my child have no father,"
that is, the nineteenth century is with us still, daddy the
general will come out of his study with an icon and curse her
(or without an icon—I don't know how they cursed people
then), the maids will drag the baby off to a foundling place
or to a wet nurse in the country. . . .

Eventually the mother-to-be decides not to have an abor-
tion, and presumably the birth of her child is meant to
connect with the birth of Russia as a major industrial
power.

Erenburg professed to admire "Oil," claiming that it
pointed the direction in which Babel might have gone as
a writer. As a minor example of five-year plan literature,
it is not without interest, but the elements uncharacteristic
of Babel do not gel altogether successfully. None of his
subsequent stories bears much resemblance to "Oil," and
it occupies a strangely isolated position among his work.

"From five to seven our hotel, the Hotel Danton,
was borne aloft by groans of love." Thus begins "Dante
Street," the other new story published in 1934 and the
first of two set by Babel in Paris. The view presented of
the French and summed up by the narrator's friend, Jean,
is thoroughly conventional: "*Mon vieux*, in the thousand
years of our history we have created women, cuisine, and
literature. . . . That no one can deny. . . ." In this story

Babel confined himself to the first of these achievements. To start with there is a distinct echo of "My First Literary Fee," with the narrator alone in a strange city and desperate for sex: "There is no solitude more hopeless than solitude in Paris." As in the earlier story, too, he lies in his room listening to a couple making love next door. In this case, however, interest is centered not on the narrator, but on the couple themselves, Jean and Germaine, whose story was apparently suggested by a Parisian trial Babel had attended.

"Dante Street" belongs with those other works in which heterosexual relations are described in humorous vein, except that here a rather banal tragedy results. Babel extracted most fun from his eavesdropping on the regular love sessions of Jean and Germaine and from the description of the panic that ensues in the hotel bedrooms on the arrival of the police to investigate Jean's murder at "the hour of love." Compared with most of his other stories, however, the writing tends to be pedestrian and the impression left is of Babel not entirely at his artistic ease in a foreign setting.

First mentioned together with "Oil" and "Dante Street," "Froim Grach" was recommended for publication by Gorky in 1933 but did not appear until as late as 1964. The story takes place in 1919 when Moldavanka criminals are being rounded up by the Cheka with a ruthlessness that equals their own. Embodying the disappearing glory of the underworld is not Benya Krik, but Froim Grach, described as the real brains behind the activities of Odessa's "forty thousand thieves." On going unarmed to bargain with the Cheka for his men's release, however, he is summarily shot. Babel's sense of the passing of an era is conveyed through an Odessite member of the Cheka who admits that such men have no place in Soviet society but who is keenly aware of the mystique that has grown up around Froim and cannot suppress his

admiration. Though by no means one of Babel's best
stories, "Froim Grach" remains notable for his sad fare-
well to the exotic world of the Moldavanka and at the
same time to an unforgettable part of his youth.

One of the most interesting discoveries made recently by researchers into Babel's work is the substantial
fragment, "The Jewess." So far unpublished in Russian
and undated, it is thought to have been written in the
mid-1930s. The differences between this and Babel's
stories predispose one to regard it as part of a novel.
Consisting chiefly of narrative, it has a more leisurely
pace, a less compressed style, and emphasis is more on
the characters' psychology. To begin with, Esther Erlich,
the Jewess of the title, has just been widowed. Her son,
Boris, a corps commissar in the Red Cavalry, persuades
her and his sister to leave their Ukrainian village settle-
ment and join him in Moscow. Babel was here extremely
successful at achieving pathos, and the rendering of
Esther's grief is very fine. So, too, are the descriptions
of the miserable lives eked out by once wealthy relatives
and of Esther's reactions to the luxury of the train in
which she travels and to her new apartment in Moscow.
One chapter is devoted to the brief biographies of Boris
and his friend and fellow Bolshevik, Selivanov, before
the manuscript peters out with a reference to the smell of
fish, garlic, and onions that so offends the Erlichs'
Muscovite neighbors. The theme of the adaptation of a
typically Jewish family to the Soviet way of life seems to
offer great possibilities for further development, and it is
regrettable that this potentially excellent work should, for
whatever reason, be incomplete.

In August 1934 Babel made a speech at the First
Congress of Soviet Writers, which has since been much
debated. His performance was a fascinating one. Though
disliking literary gatherings of any sort, Babel obviously
felt obliged by the attacks against him to defend his point

of view. He endeavored to disarm his critics with a mélange of modesty, humor, and obeisance to the party. Erenburg had already stood up for Babel against those at the congress who deplored Babel's apparent inactivity. The older writer likened his own fertility to that of a rabbit and that of Babel to an elephant, which required a longer gestation period. Babel duly acknowledged Erenburg's support, confessing himself a master of the genre of silence, but said he had too great a respect for the reader to foist on him work that was badly written.

With the exception of *Maria*, published in March 1935, Babel maintained his "masterful" silence, and no new stories by him appeared either in this or the following year. In a letter of February 1935 he wrote to his mother of having undergone a strange change that had left him unable to write stories and turned him toward drama. Mention is made of the slow progress of a stage comedy, but no details are given.

In June 1935 Babel left for Paris as a delegate to the Congress for the Defense of Peace and Culture but could not stay long and returned later in the summer. This was the last time he saw his relatives abroad. September found him in Odessa where he stayed about six weeks gathering strength before moving to Moscow. By the end of the year he was living with Antonina Pirozhkov, a devoted companion for the rest of his days, who bore him a daughter in January 1937.

Babel again saw fit to defend his silence at a literary conference in 1936, but the biggest blow to him during that year was the death of Gorky three months later. Lost was a powerful friend and protector, and from this time on Babel's safety became increasingly precarious. In August, however, he was again in Odessa, where his writing always progressed more smoothly and where, apart from a three-week absence in Yalta on film business, he remained until late November. An ironic incident was the loss of a favorite pocket watch, stolen from him on a streetcar—an example of poetic justice, considering how he had exploited his knowledge of the local thieves!

In 1937 three new stories appeared by Babel—his first for three years. "Sulak" is very short and written for the most part in a plain, straightforward style. The narrative concerns the tracking down of an anti-Soviet bandit who had escaped in 1922 but whose presence in the Ukrainian countryside is reported six years later. The most memorable feature of the story is the dwarfishness of Sulak's wife. Since her husband's disappearance she has produced several children and is eventually discovered to be hiding him in a concealed hole. Apart from this example of the grotesque, however, Babel does not aim at any particularly striking effects, and the story is one of his more mediocre.

"Di Grasso" finds Babel returned to more familiar territory—the Odessa he knew before World War I. This story encompasses two streams that finally converge. On the one hand the fourteen-year-old narrator tells how the Sicilian tragedian, Di Grasso, took the city by storm after his troupe had made an unpromising start. The sparse first-night audience is totally won over by a remarkable leap from Di Grasso himself, who, playing the part of a Sicilian shepherd, bites through the throat and sucks out the blood of his rival in love. From this point on, the company's success is assured, and Di Grasso, acclaimed by Odessites the actor of the century, asserts "by his every word and gesture that in the ecstasy of noble passion there is more hope and justice than in the joyless rules of this world."

The second stream, on the other hand, involves the narrator's adolescent misery. All ends well, however, thanks to Di Grasso. Overcome by emotion after Di Grasso's last performance, the wife of the man who has brought the narrator grief persuades her husband to set matters right. Thus art influences and ennobles life. It is Babel's view of art as expressed and embodied in "Di Grasso" that most lingers in the memory, and for this reason the story has always been among the most popular of his later works.

In "The Kiss" Babel also returned to familiar terrain. The setting is that of *Red Cavalry*, and the narrator, like Lyutov, an officer and former law graduate. Budyonny's Polish campaign, however, merely serves as a backdrop to a love affair. The narrator's attempt to seduce Elizaveta, widowed daughter of a paralyzed schoolmaster, is aided by his wily Cossack orderly but interrupted by the call of duty. When the campaign later brings the narrator near Elizaveta's home again, he utilizes the opportunity to consummate the relationship, being finally rescued by his orderly, who fears lest his master become too entangled. Babel remained dissatisfied with this story, which lacks the color of most of his *Red Cavalry* work and fails to make anything extraordinary of the romantic theme. Indeed, one is tempted to regard it as an example on Babel's part of the dangers of excessive eagerness to forsake the genre of silence.

In September 1937 Babel was questioned about his silence, among other things, by an audience assembled by the Union of Soviet Writers. At first in a self-disparaging way he spoke of his unsuitability as a writer and then went on to mention, as one would expect, his fastidiousness and reluctance to put ideas on paper in a hurry. Many of his answers, indeed, make strange reading. Asked about his favorite authors, he mentioned neither Gogol nor Maupassant, referring instead to Pushkin, Tolstoy, and Sholokhov, presumably because he considered them more acceptable to his questioners. In an allusion to his chosen medium, he confessed having tried without success to write at greater length and in a more weighty way, but whereas Tolstoy was capable of describ-

ing every minute of every day, he himself could only pick
out the most interesting five minutes. The general impression is of a man walking a tightrope, but trying to
be as sincere as difficult circumstances would permit.
Significantly no account of this meeting appeared in the
Soviet Union until April 1964.

The last of Babel's new works to appear in the Soviet
Union before his death was "The Trial," published in
1938. In this slight story, too, Babel did not show himself at his best. The main objects of his satire are French
legal procedure and a former White officer who has been
unable to settle down since emigrating and receives a ten-
year prison sentence for stealing from an elderly woman.
He understands nothing of what is being said at his trial:
"Helpless and huge, his arms hanging down, he towered
above the crowd like a mournful animal from another
world." Moreover, after sentence has been passed with
cheerful briskness, he simply does not know what has
happened. Babel's love of the grotesque is much in evidence in "The Trial," but the story, which lacks shape
and ends flatly, hardly provided a worthy end to his
literary career.

During the last few years prior to his arrest, Babel
was occupied mainly with film work, which appealed to
him no more than before. Viktor Shklovsky gives a sad
picture of him in 1937: "Babel was walking quietly and
dejectedly and spoke of the cinema. He appeared very
tired, spoke softly, and simply could not tie up and finish
whatever it was he wanted to say."

The last letter Babel sent his mother and sister is
dated 10 May 1939. Five days later he was arrested and
for several years his fate remained in doubt. Not until
1954 was his trial by military court in 1940 confirmed
and a certificate issued showing that he had died of an
unspecified cause on 17 March 1941.

8

Babel

the Artist

Contemplating the career of Babel, one is left, as in the case of other gifted Soviet writers, with a feeling of waste and with a number of hypothetical questions. What else would he have accomplished, given favorable working conditions, during the period of his artistic maturity? How would his talents have burgeoned had he survived the purges to enjoy a normal span of life? Such questions remain as imponderable as the quality and nature of the work, created during the 1930s, that has apparently fallen into limbo. Nevertheless, it is only fair to pose them before pronouncing on his art as we know it.

It is easier to say what Babel was *not* as a writer. He continued few traditions of Russian literature of the nineteenth century and left admirers but no disciples in the twentieth. He did not deal with complex human problems and abstract ideas in the manner of a Tolstoy or Pasternak, or with contemporary events like a Turgenev or Erenburg. Apart from some early pieces of journalism, his work seems almost totally lacking in moral seriousness. He attempted little psychological analysis ("The Jewess" is the most interesting exception) and certainly none in the manner of a Dostoyevsky or of Soviet writers influenced by Dostoyevsky's genius. Though the content of many of Babel's stories absorbs the reader by virtue of fascinating and unfamiliar backgrounds, he was primarily a superb stylist with a limited form and a limited range who regarded pure content as secondary.

Babel's faith in style was one of the few faiths he possessed. Born a Jew, he rejected the creed of his fathers. Caught up in revolution, he did not become a member of the only party the state permitted. Wary of belonging, he often seems in his work reluctant to admit to membership of the absurd human race. Paustovsky described him as "outwardly inclined toward skepticism, even toward cynicism." The authentic voice of Babel's cynicism can be heard speaking through an emaciated old man in "The End of the Poorhouse": "Life's a dung-heap, . . . the world a brothel, and people a bunch of crooks."

Despite Paustovsky's reassurance that Babel really believed in a naive and good human soul, he was, on the evidence of his work, hardly enamored of people. The great Russian literary vice of sentimentality is almost entirely absent from his writings (though, of course, he was not a Russian but a Ukrainian, and a Jew with cosmopolitan tendencies, to boot). If he lacks sentimentality, neither is he blessed with an abundance of sentiment. Characters tend to be ironically, grotesquely, cruelly drawn. Often there is little or no trace of sympathy for people placed in a fearful predicament. Usually they appear to exist less as objects of human interest than for their usefulness in enabling the author to exhibit his literary skills. This suggests a basic heartlessness, as too, do Babel's working methods and his obsession with surface polish. Hardly anything in his work seems spontaneous and straight from the heart. The real Babel lies buried under piles of variants. One feels closer to him in his letters to his mother and sister, but even then his mindfulness of the censor inhibits.

Much of Babel's humor derives from human foibles, monstrously swollen in presentation. It is often meant to shock, as, too, are details and situations involving sex and violence. There is something of the awful schoolboy about Babel's passion for sacrilege, which constituted for him an artistic way of life and an integral part of the "small and terrible" world in many of his stories and both his plays. This world has small proportions because he prefers to be a miniaturist as regards literary form and to examine an extraordinary segment of a given situation instead of its totality. The vantage point resulting from such an approach can also shock by its incongruity. All these characteristics combine to make Babel among the least dull as well as the least edifying of writers.

Despite Babel's intellectual renunciation of Judaism, his best works owe much to the tension generated by his Jewishness. A wryness essentially Jewish in nature permeates his art, even though the Jewishness may sometimes be *sotto voce*.

It was to art that Babel dedicated himself from childhood. According to Paustovsky, he could not decide whether to regard it as an angel or a demon. According to Nathalie Babel, "his life centered on writing, and it can be said without exaggeration that he sacrificed everything to his art, including his relationship with his family, his liberty, and finally even his life." But despite such commitment, despite his political rehabilitation, and despite his popularity with the Soviet reading public, no complete set of Babel's works has been issued yet, some thirty years after his death. Had he foreseen such a fate, even one of the finest ironists known to Russian literature is unlikely to have been amused.

By Way of an Afterword: Quotations from Babel

On Revolution

"To the Revolution we will say 'yes,' but must we say 'no' to the Sabbath? . . . 'Yes' I cry to the Revolution. 'Yes' I cry to it. But it hides from Gedali and sends forth nothing but gunfire." ("Gedali," *Red Cavalry*.)

"You shoot because you are the Revolution. But does not Revolution bring joy? And does not joy hate to see orphans in a home? Good deeds are done by good men. Revolution is the good deed of good men. But good men do not murder. So the Revolution is being made by bad men. But the Poles are also bad men. Who then can tell Gedali where lies revolution and where lies counterrevolution?" ("Gedali," *Red Cavalry*.)

On Politics

"We are no ignoramuses. The International—we know what the International is. And I want an International of good people. . . . ("Gedali," *Red Cavalry*.)

Loudly, like a deaf man in his hour of triumph, I read out Lenin's speech to the Cossacks.

103

The evening swathed me in the life-giving dampness of its dusky sheets; the evening lay the palms of a mother on my burning brow. I read and rejoiced and, as I rejoiced, tried to anticipate the mysterious curve in Lenin's straight line. ("My First Goose," *Red Cavalry*.)

On Religious Feeling

Then the singing of the organ struck my ear, and at the same moment an old woman appeared in the doorway of our headquarters, her yellow hair loose and flowing. Reeling and stumbling, she moved like a dog with a broken paw. Tears gushed from her eyes, which were suffused with the white moisture of blindness. The sounds from the organ floated toward us, sometimes scurrying, sometimes painfully slow. They flew to us with difficulty, leaving behind a persistently plaintive ring. The old woman wiped away the tears with her yellow hair, sat down on the ground and began to kiss my boots at the knee. The organ fell silent and then began to chortle raucously on the base notes. ("In Saint Valentine's Church," *Red Cavalry*.)

In this temple of Berestechko an original and enticing point of view had been expressed on the mortal sufferings of the sons of men. In this temple saints went to their execution as picturesquely as Italian opera singers, and the black hair of the executioners was as glossy as the beard of Holophernes. ("In Saint Valentine's Church," *Red Cavalry*.)

Pan Lyudomirsky, clad in a green frock coat, was standing beneath the statue. Stretching forth a withered hand, he began to curse us. The Cossacks goggled and hung their straw-colored forelocks. With a voice like thunder the bell ringer of St. Valentine's Church was pronouncing anathema in purest Latin. Then he turned away, fell on his knees and embraced the feet of the Savior. ("In Saint Valentine's Church," *Red Cavalry*.)

On War

The transport wagons were racing along, roaring and sinking in the mud. The morning seeped out onto us, like chloroform onto an operating table.

"Are you married, Lyutov?" all of a sudden asked Volkov, who was sitting at the back.

"My wife has left me," I replied, dozed off for a few moments and dreamed that I was sleeping in a proper bed.

Silence.

Our horse was stumbling.

"The mare will be fagged out in another mile or two," said Volkov, who was sitting at the back.

Silence.

"We've lost the campaign," mumbled Volkov and let out a snore.

"Yes," I said. (The final lines of "Zamost'ye," *Red Cavalry*.)

The village swam and swelled, the purple clay flowing from its dreary wounds. The first star flashed above me and disappeared down into the storm clouds. The rain whipped the white willows and then became impotent. The evening flew up to the sky, like a flock of birds, and the darkness placed upon me its wet garland. Bent and exhausted beneath this sepulchral crown, I walked on, imploring from fate that simplest of abilities—the ability to take a human life. ("After the Battle," *Red Cavalry*.)

On Being a Jew

Of Peter the Great I knew by heart from Putsykovich's book and the poetry of Pushkin. Sobbing all the while, I recited this poetry. Suddenly human faces rolled down into my eyes and shuffled about there, like cards from a new pack. They shuffled about at the base of my eyes, and at these moments I shuddered, pulled myself up straight, and

hurriedly declaimed Pushkin's stanzas at the top of my voice.
I declaimed them for a long time, and no one interrupted my
crazy muttering. Through a purple blindness, through the
feeling of liberation that had gripped me, I could see only
the aged, inclined face of Pyatnitsky with its silver-speckled
beard. . . .

"What a nation," whispered the old man. "These little
Yids of yours—there's the devil in them." ("The Story of
My Dovecote.")

On Anti-Semitism

The peasant made me take a light from his.

"The Yids are to blame for everything," he said. "For
what's happened to us and for what's happened to you. After
the war there'll be precious few of them left. How many Yids
are there altogether in the world?"

"Ten million," I replied and began bridling my horse.

"Two hundred thousand is all that'll be left of them,"
cried the peasant and touched me on the arm, afraid lest I
should go. But I managed to climb into the saddle and set
off at a gallop to where our headquarters had been set up.
("Zamost'ye," *Red Cavalry.*)

On Russian Vodka

At our ball everyone was gay. Even mother sipped some
vodka, though she didn't like it and couldn't understand
those who did. For this reason she regarded all Russians as
madmen and couldn't conceive how women brought themselves to live with Russian husbands. ("The Story of My
Dovecote.")

On Friendship

And so we lost Khlebnikov. I was very grieved, for
Khlebnikov was a quiet chap with a character similar to

mine. He alone in the squadron possessed a samovar. Whenever there was a lull we would drink hot tea together. And he would tell me stories about women with such a wealth of detail that I found it both shameful and agreeable to listen to him. This, I believe, was because we were moved by identical passions. Both of us regarded the world as a meadow in May, a meadow through which pass women and horses. ("The Story of a Horse," *Red Cavalry*.)

On Lovemaking

Their regular days were Wednesday and Sunday. She used to come at five o'clock. A moment later their room would resound with groaning, with the thud of falling bodies, with exclamations of alarm, and then would begin that sweet agony of womankind.

"Oh, Jean . . ."

I used to calculate to myself. Germaine has gone in now. She has closed the door behind her. They have had their kiss. The girl has taken off her hat and gloves and put them on the table. According to my calculations no more time remained. There wasn't long enough to undress. Without uttering a single word, they would be leaping about between the sheets like a pair of hares. Having groaned awhile, they would kill themselves laughing and babble of their affairs. About this I knew everything a neighbor can know who is living behind a wood partition. ("Dante Street.")

On Laughter

"The jackal howls when it is hungry. Any fool has folly enough to be downcast, but only a wise man can tear apart with laughter the veil of existence." ("The Rabbi," *Red Cavalry*.)

On Writing

"Only a genius can permit himself two adjectives with a single noun." (Babel, quoted by Konstantin Paustovsky in Book IV of *The Story of My Life.*)

He read my writings, twitched a shoulder, ran a hand through his stern, gray curls, and paced up and down the attic.

"There is reason to suppose," he articulated slowly, pausing after every word, "that you do have some sort of divine spark. . . ." ("Awakening.)"

Bibliography

The years given are those of initial publication, generally in literary journals and newspapers. If no year follows the Russian title, then the work has appeared only in translation.

1. Works by Isaac Babel

Argamak. *Argamak*, 1932.
Awakening. *Probuzhdeniye*, 1931.
Bagrat-Ogly and the Eyes of His Bull. *Bagrat-Ogly i glaza ego byka*, 1923.
The Beast Is Silent. *Zver' molchit*, 1918.
The Blind Men. *Slepye*, 1918.
Childhood: At Grandmother's. *Detstvo. U babushki*, 1965.
Chinky Chinaman. *Khódya*, 1923.
Dante Street. *Ulitsa Dante*, 1934.
The Deserter. *Dezertir*, 1920.
Di Grasso. *Di Grasso*, 1937.
Doudou. *Doudou*, 1917.
The End of the Poorhouse. *Konets bogadel'ni*, 1932.
The End of Saint Hypatius. *Konets sv. Ipatiya*, 1924.
Evacuees. *Evakuyirovannye*, 1918.
Evening. *Vecher*, 1918.
An Evening at the Empress's. *Vecher u imperatritsy*, 1922.

109

Premature Babies. *Nedonoski*, 1918.
The Public Library. *Publichnaya bibliyoteka*, 1916.
The Quaker. *Kvaker*, 1920.
Red Cavalry. *Konarmiya*, 1923–25.
Shabos-Nahamu. *Shabos-Nahamu*, 1918.
The Sin of Jesus. *Lyisusov grekh*, 1924.
The S.S. *Cow-Wheat*. *Ivan-da-Mar'ya*, 1932.
The Story of My Dovecote. *Istoriya moyey golubyatni*, 1925.
Story of a Woman. *Skazka pro babu*, 1923.
Sulak. *Sulak*, 1937.
Sunset (the play). *Zakat*, 1928.
Sunset (the story). *Zakat*, 1964.
There Were Nine of Them, 1970. *Ikh bylo devyat'*.
Through the Fanlight. *V shcholochku*, 1923.
The Trial. *Sud*, 1938.
With Our Leader Makhno. *U bat'ki nashego Makhno*, 1924.
You Were Taken In, Captain. *Ty promorgal, kapitan*, 1924.

2. Russian Selected Works

Izbrannoye. Moscow, 1966.

3. English Translations of Babel's Works

Harland, J. *Red Cavalry*. London, 1929.
Hayward, M. *You Must Know Everything*. New York, 1969.
MacAndrew, A. R. *Lyubka the Cossack, and Other Stories*. New York, 1963.
MacAndrew, A. R. and Hayward, M. *Isaac Babel. The Lonely Years 1925–39*. New York, 1964.
Morison, W. *Collected Stories*. New York, 1955. Includes *Red Cavalry, Tales of Odessa*, and selected stories.

4.   *Western Works about Babel*

Brodal, J. "Fathers and Sons. Isaac Babel and the Generation Conflict." *Scando-Slavica* 17 (1971) : 27–43.

Carden, P. *The Art of Isaac Babel.* Ithaca and London, 1972.

Falen, J. "A Note on the Fate of Isaac Babel." *Slavic and East European Journal,* no. 4 (1967), pp. 398–404.

Murphy, A. B. "The Style of Isaac Babel." *Slavonic and East European Review,* no. 103 (1966), pp. 361–80.

Poggioli, R. "Isaac Babel in Retrospect." In *The Phoenix and the Spider,* pp. 229–38. Harvard University, 1957.

Stora-Sandor, J. *Isaac Babel. L'homme et l'oeuvre.* Paris, 1968.

Trilling, L. Introduction to *Collected Stories.* New York, 1955.

Index